BEADED EMBROIDERY
STITCHING

CHRISTEN BROWN

125 Stitches to Embellish with Beads, Buttons, Charms, Bead Weaving & More; 8+ Projects

C&T PUBLISHING

Text copyright © 2019 by Christen Brown

Photography and artwork copyright © 2019 by C&T Publishing, Inc.

Publisher: Amy Marson

Creative Director: Gailen Runge

Acquisitions Editor: Roxane Cerda

Managing Editor: Liz Aneloski

Editor: Katie Van Amburg

Technical Editor: Helen Frost

Cover/Book Designer: April Mostek

Production Coordinator: Tim Manibusan

Production Editor: Jennifer Warren

Illustrator: Mary E. Flynn

Photo Assistants: Mai Yong Vang and Rachel Holmes

Cover photography by Mai Yong Vang of C&T Publishing, Inc.

Quilt photography by Mai Yong Vang and subject photography by Kelly Burgoyne of C&T Publishing, Inc.

Published by C&T Publishing, Inc., P.O. Box 1456, Lafayette, CA 94549

Library of Congress Cataloging-in-Publication Data

Names: Brown, Christen (Christen Joan), author.

Title: Beaded embroidery stitching : 125 stitches to embellish with beads, buttons, charms, bead weaving & more; 8+ projects / Christen Brown.

Description: Lafayette, CA : C&T Publishing, Inc., [2019] | Includes bibliographical references and index.

Identifiers: LCCN 2018037410 | ISBN 9781617456732 (softcover : alk. paper)

Subjects: LCSH: Bead embroidery. | Beadwork--Patterns.

Classification: LCC TT860 .B75 2019 | DDC 745.58/2--dc23

LC record available at https://lccn.loc.gov/2018037410

Printed in the USA

10 9 8 7 6

SPECIAL ACKNOWLEDGMENTS

I have been fortunate to have the most wonderful people helping me throughout the process of designing, writing, editing, and photographing this book. I would like to thank each and every person whose expertise has touched these pages. Special thanks go to Liz and Katie, my editors—you know how special you are, and I do appreciate you.

Thank you also to those who bequeathed their precious bits of lace, fabric, trims, and buttons to me. I have enjoyed giving them a permanent home in my creations.

Beaded Tandletons variation

Autumn Buttons Bracelet

HAPPY CREATING

I dedicate this book to all of my students, both
past and present. Thank you for giving me this
opportunity to share my knowledge with you.
May you always find the time to enjoy
the creative adventure.

One-Hour Flower

CONTENTS

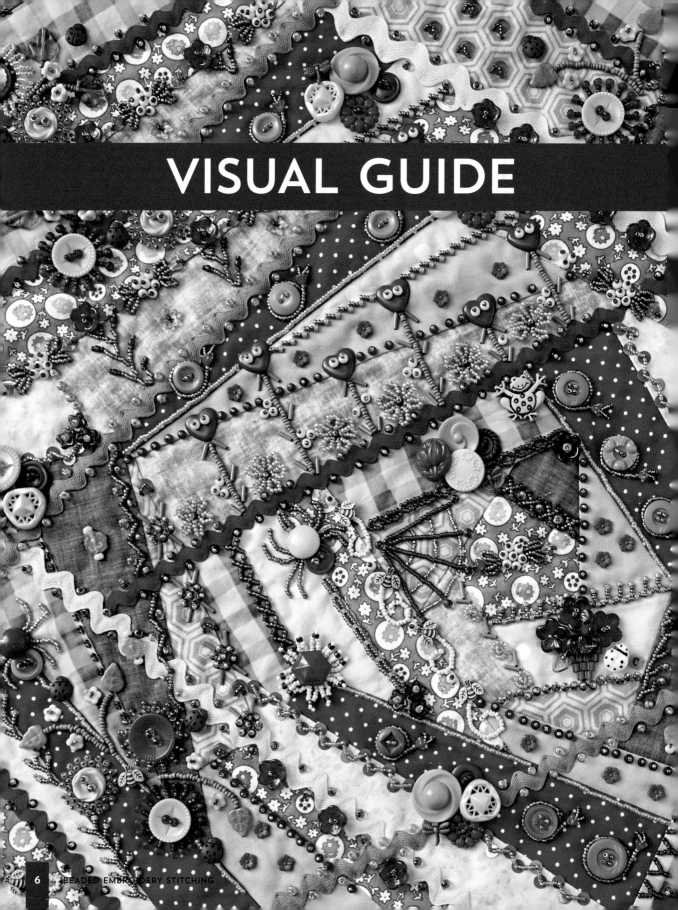

VISUAL GUIDE

LAZY DAISY AND CHAIN STITCHES

The lazy daisy stitch can be stitched as a single unit or shape or can be repeated to create a border row.
The chain stitch can be stitched as a border row or used to outline a shape.

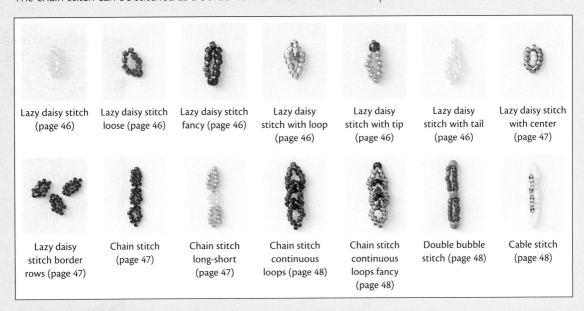

Lazy daisy stitch (page 46)

Lazy daisy stitch loose (page 46)

Lazy daisy stitch fancy (page 46)

Lazy daisy stitch with loop (page 46)

Lazy daisy stitch with tip (page 46)

Lazy daisy stitch with tail (page 46)

Lazy daisy stitch with center (page 47)

Lazy daisy stitch border rows (page 47)

Chain stitch (page 47)

Chain stitch long-short (page 47)

Chain stitch continuous loops (page 48)

Chain stitch continuous loops fancy (page 48)

Double bubble stitch (page 48)

Cable stitch (page 48)

FLY AND FEATHER STITCHES

The fly stitch can be stitched as a single unit or shape or can be repeated to create a border row. The feather
stitch can be stitched as a border row or used to outline a shape.

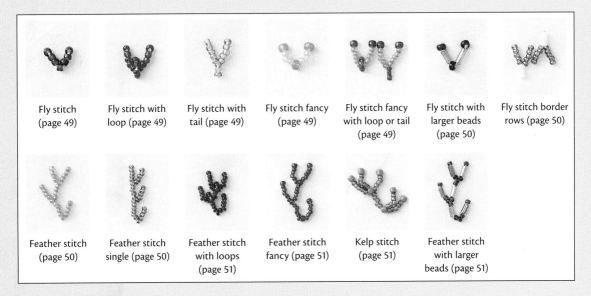

Fly stitch (page 49)

Fly stitch with loop (page 49)

Fly stitch with tail (page 49)

Fly stitch fancy (page 49)

Fly stitch fancy with loop or tail (page 49)

Fly stitch with larger beads (page 50)

Fly stitch border rows (page 50)

Feather stitch (page 50)

Feather stitch single (page 50)

Feather stitch with loops (page 51)

Feather stitch fancy (page 51)

Kelp stitch (page 51)

Feather stitch with larger beads (page 51)

Primarily Crazy for Kevin, project inspiration for CQ Sewing Caddy (page 132)

CONTINUOUS BEAD AND BLANKET STITCHES

The continuous bead and blanket stitches can be stitched as a border row or used to outline a shape.

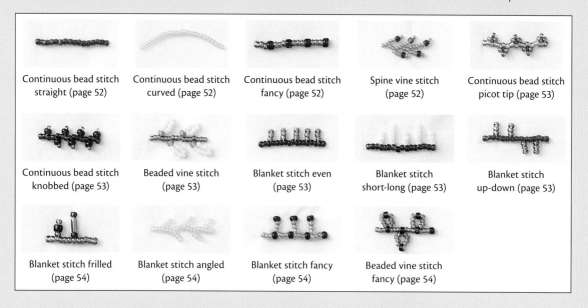

Continuous bead stitch straight (page 52)

Continuous bead stitch curved (page 52)

Continuous bead stitch fancy (page 52)

Spine vine stitch (page 52)

Continuous bead stitch picot tip (page 53)

Continuous bead stitch knobbed (page 53)

Beaded vine stitch (page 53)

Blanket stitch even (page 53)

Blanket stitch short-long (page 53)

Blanket stitch up-down (page 53)

Blanket stitch frilled (page 54)

Blanket stitch angled (page 54)

Blanket stitch fancy (page 54)

Beaded vine stitch fancy (page 54)

CROSS, HERRINGBONE, SERPENTINE, AND CRETAN STITCHES

The cross stitch can be used as a single unit or as a border row. The herringbone, serpentine, and cretan stitches can be used as a border row stitch.

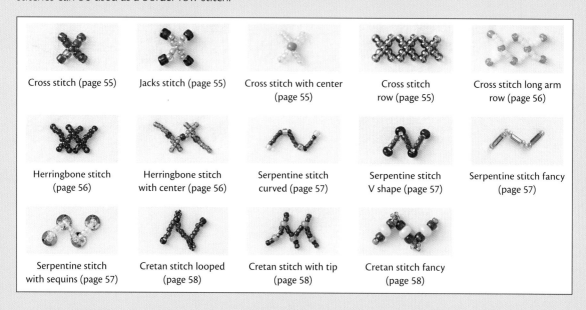

Cross stitch (page 55)

Jacks stitch (page 55)

Cross stitch with center (page 55)

Cross stitch row (page 55)

Cross stitch long arm row (page 56)

Herringbone stitch (page 56)

Herringbone stitch with center (page 56)

Serpentine stitch curved (page 57)

Serpentine stitch V shape (page 57)

Serpentine stitch fancy (page 57)

Serpentine stitch with sequins (page 57)

Cretan stitch looped (page 58)

Cretan stitch with tip (page 58)

Cretan stitch fancy (page 58)

FLOWERS AND EXTRA STITCHES

These are all individual stitches that can placed into an open area or grouped together as a vignette.

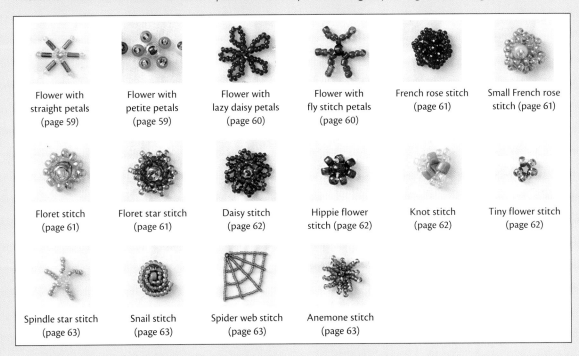

Flower with straight petals (page 59)

Flower with petite petals (page 59)

Flower with lazy daisy petals (page 60)

Flower with fly stitch petals (page 60)

French rose stitch (page 61)

Small French rose stitch (page 61)

Floret stitch (page 61)

Floret star stitch (page 61)

Daisy stitch (page 62)

Hippie flower stitch (page 62)

Knot stitch (page 62)

Tiny flower stitch (page 62)

Spindle star stitch (page 63)

Snail stitch (page 63)

Spider web stitch (page 63)

Anemone stitch (page 63)

DECORATIVE AND DETAIL STITCHES

These stitches can be worked as a single unit, grouped together in a cluster, or used as a border row.

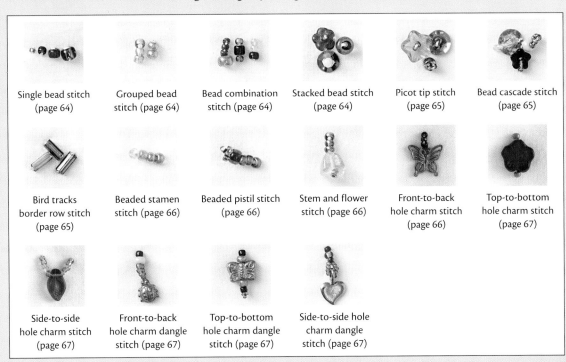

Single bead stitch (page 64)

Grouped bead stitch (page 64)

Bead combination stitch (page 64)

Stacked bead stitch (page 64)

Picot tip stitch (page 65)

Bead cascade stitch (page 65)

Bird tracks border row stitch (page 65)

Beaded stamen stitch (page 66)

Beaded pistil stitch (page 66)

Stem and flower stitch (page 66)

Front-to-back hole charm stitch (page 66)

Top-to-bottom hole charm stitch (page 67)

Side-to-side hole charm stitch (page 67)

Front-to-back hole charm dangle stitch (page 67)

Top-to-bottom hole charm dangle stitch (page 67)

Side-to-side hole charm dangle stitch (page 67)

BUTTON AND SEQUIN FLOWERS

These are all individual stitches that can be stitched here and there or grouped together as vignettes.

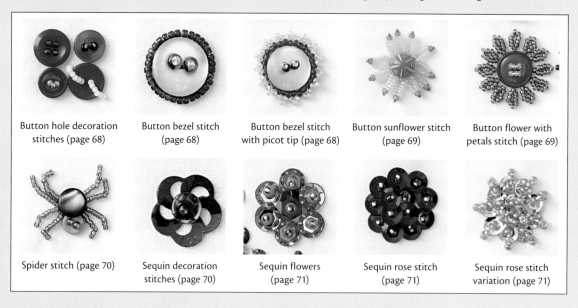

Button hole decoration stitches (page 68)

Button bezel stitch (page 68)

Button bezel stitch with picot tip (page 68)

Button sunflower stitch (page 69)

Button flower with petals stitch (page 69)

Spider stitch (page 70)

Sequin decoration stitches (page 70)

Sequin flowers (page 71)

Sequin rose stitch (page 71)

Sequin rose stitch variation (page 71)

BEADED EDGES

These stitches can be added to the finished edge of a project to add a little sparkle.

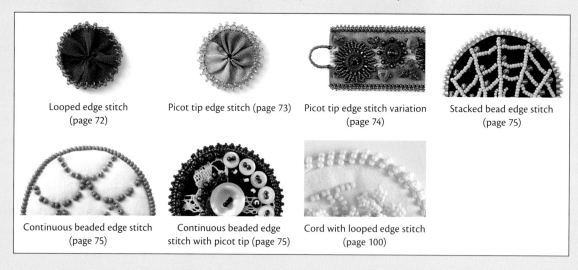

Looped edge stitch (page 72)

Picot tip edge stitch (page 73)

Picot tip edge stitch variation (page 74)

Stacked bead edge stitch (page 75)

Continuous beaded edge stitch (page 75)

Continuous beaded edge stitch with picot tip (page 75)

Cord with looped edge stitch (page 100)

EVEN PEYOTE AND FREE-FORM PEYOTE STITCHES

These stitches are worked onto the fabric following a straight or curved line.

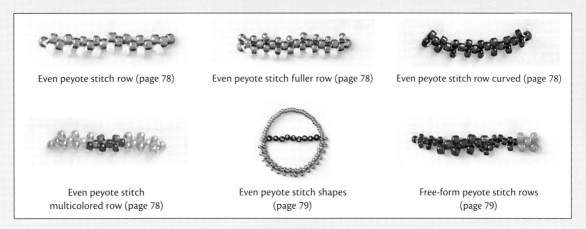

Even peyote stitch row (page 78)   Even peyote stitch fuller row (page 78)   Even peyote stitch row curved (page 78)

Even peyote stitch
multicolored row (page 78)

Even peyote stitch shapes
(page 79)

Free-form peyote stitch rows
(page 79)

CIRCULAR PEYOTE AND NETTED STITCHES

These stitches are worked as individual units and then attached to the fabric base.

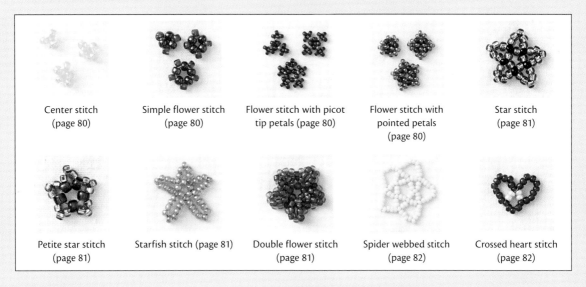

Center stitch
(page 80)

Simple flower stitch
(page 80)

Flower stitch with picot
tip petals (page 80)

Flower stitch with
pointed petals
(page 80)

Star stitch
(page 81)

Petite star stitch
(page 81)

Starfish stitch (page 81)

Double flower stitch
(page 81)

Spider webbed stitch
(page 82)

Crossed heart stitch
(page 82)

BRICK STITCH

These stitches are worked as individual units and then attached to the fabric base.

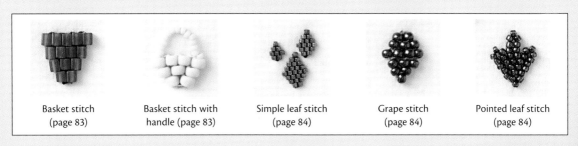

Basket stitch
(page 83)

Basket stitch with
handle (page 83)

Simple leaf stitch
(page 84)

Grape stitch
(page 84)

Pointed leaf stitch
(page 84)

BEADY-EYED FROM THE START

GROWING UP IN THE 60S

I have loved beads for as long as I can remember. As a kid, I would play dress-up with my grandmother's jewelry, pretending that I was getting ready for a fancy dinner party. My neck and arms would be draped in layers of pearls and glass beads, and I would clip her earrings onto my ears and clothing. To complete my ensemble, I would choose a hat, gloves, and an evening bag.

Grandmother's glass pearl necklace and earrings, sequin hat, bead and sequin handbag, and crochet gloves

Through grade school and high school, I belonged to an organization called Camp Fire Girls, which provided social and community experiences for young people. We completed tasks in areas like science, sports, citizenship, and home sciences.

Each task was rewarded with a wooden bead that corresponded to the color of the task.

Other achievements in growth were rewarded with an embroidered badge and, upon graduation to the next level of the program, a piece of jewelry. The beads and badges were first sewn onto a wool vest and eventually onto a ceremonial gown. The design and display of one's achievements were left up to each individual.

Camp Fire Girls beads, jewelry, scarf, hankies, and newspaper clipping

During Camp Fire Girls and high school arts and crafts classes, I also learned how to make projects on a small bead loom. The loomed projects would use glass seed beads that came in glass vials or that were temporarily strung in a group and wrapped in wax paper.

Vintage glass bead vials and loose beads

VINTAGE BEAD EMBROIDERY AND BEAD WEAVING

Those early influences changed my life in so many ways and left a fascination for beads that is still strong. I inherited my grandmother's jewelry and other accessories. I also collect items from garage sales, thrift stores, and online. I am particularly drawn to jewelry and handbags, but, of course, all manner of "beady treasures" catch my eye.

During the early part of the twentieth century and even today, jewelry designers have used beads in a variety of shapes, sizes, and materials in their creations. Early designs often included realistic shapes such as flowers and leaves. Occasionally, you will find buttons with shanks that have been strung onto beading thread to create a necklace or bracelet.

The items above were all made using flower and leaf shapes in either plastic or glass. The cream-colored necklace and pastel-colored bracelet began with bone rings for the base of the design.

The pieces of jewelry on the left were made from a variety of techniques and materials, including bead woven techniques, crochet, and wire work.

The two beaded necklaces are comprised of strands of beads that have been braided; one has a bead-woven stitched flower worked into one strand. The first bracelet was crocheted with beads strung onto a fine thread, and the second bracelet was worked using a bead woven technique called right-angle weave. The earrings were beaded onto a fine wire and attached to a metal finding.

The two images at the top of the page are details of purses that were embroidered with threads and beads (strung on thread) using a tambour needle. Tambour embroidery is a continuous worked chain stitch formed on the fabric with the thread held underneath in one hand while the other hand inserts the hook down through the fabric to catch the thread.

The design on each of the two purses below has been embroidered with glass beads and sequins. Notice the shapes and patterns of the sequins. Both of these purses have a little strap sewn to the back of the bag to slip your hand through.

BEADS, CLASSES, AND MORE BEADS!

My creative journey through bead embroidery and bead weaving has been a long and happy adventure. I am lucky to be able to teach the joys of these tiny wonderful treasures, as it brings me a great sense of pleasure and satisfaction.

The beadazzled vest on the left is an example from one of the first classes that I taught using bead embroidery. It begins with a piece of tapestry fabric for the base, which is backed with iron-on interfacing to give the fabric stability. Ten stitches were included in the instructions.

Guinevere's Garden

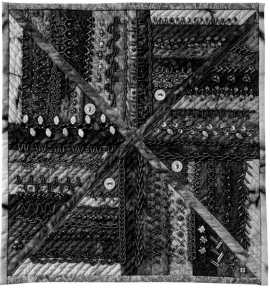

Beadazzled Stitches

The vest class eventually evolved into a four-week program, covering a more extensive list of stitches. The base above was strip pieced, backed with batting for stability, and machine quilted.

I have also been lucky enough to teach several jewelry classes using many bead woven techniques. The bracelet on the right features the pointed leaf stitch (page 84) on a beaded base.

Spiral Vine Bracelet (See the gallery example, page 142.)

Free-form peyote stitched bracelet

I began experimenting with the free-form peyote stitch for jewelry. I really enjoyed this technique, though I often found that the tension presented a problem for students, which meant that the beaded rows were either too loose or too tight.

Ocean Rivers, free-form peyote stitched bracelet

I adapted the free-form peyote technique to be used on a fiber base—in this instance, a piece of ribbon. The solid fiber base allowed for a more even, firmer row of stitches, relieving any wonkiness or unevenness. The beading began in rows of the continuous stitch similar to those of The Stars are Out Tonight (page 112).

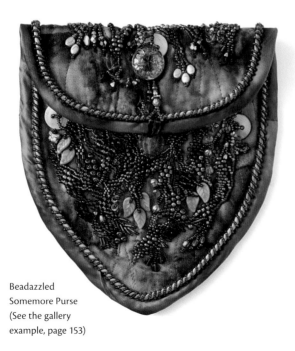
Beadazzled Somemore Purse (See the gallery example, page 153)

This purse is another example of the free-form peyote stitch on a fiber base—in this case, a batik fabric. The fabric was backed with batting and quilted in a random pattern. The beading began with curved free-form peyote stitch rows (page 79).

BEADS AND EMBELLISHMENTS: CANDY WITH NO CALORIES!

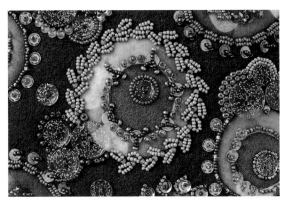

Detail of Blowing Bubbles: Jewel Bubbles project (See full photo and project instructions, page 121.)

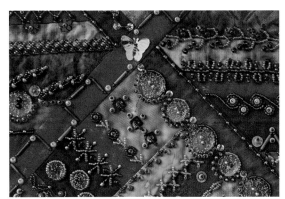

Detail of *Sizzle and Pop* (page 152)

Glass Flowers, project inspiration for Beaded Bracelets (page 108)

Beads, buttons, charms, sequins, and other embellishments come in a variety of shapes, sizes, colors, and finishes. Once you begin to collect these items, your imagination will ignite, and the ideas will start to flow. I suggest that you make time for a "play day" at least once a week so that you can explore the possibilities!

TINY, SHINY TREASURES!

Initially the word *bead* brings to mind sparkling little round wonders of light and color, but beads come in many different shapes and sizes. Seed beads are numbered from low to high: the higher the number, the smaller the bead. Bugle beads are numbered in millimeters.

Shapes and Sizes

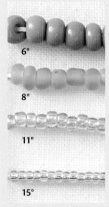

Size 6°, 8°, 11°, and 15° seed beads

Round seed beads, or *rocailles,* are round and even in shape and come in sizes 5° to 18°; some vintage beads can be found as small as size 24°. These beads, referred to as *SBs* in embroidery tables in this book, can be worked effectively into any of the bead embroidery and bead woven stitches.

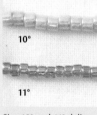

Size 10° and 11° delica beads

Cylinder beads, called *delica* or *antiques,* are tube shaped and come in sizes 8° to 11°. The shape and consistent size make them perfect for the peyote and brick stitch designs, but they can also be used for the bead embroidery stitches.

Size 8° and 12° cut beads

Cut beads are round in shape, with one or several sides squared off to create sparkle. They come in sizes 8° to 15°. These beads can be worked effectively into any of the bead embroidery and bead woven stitches.

Size 8° and 15° hex cut beads

Hex cut beads are six sided and come in sizes 5° to 15°. These beads can be worked effectively into any of the bead embroidery and bead woven stitches.

Size 4° and 11° square beads

Square beads have four sides and come in sizes 4° to 15°. The shape and consistent size make them perfect for the peyote and brick stitch designs, but they can also be used for the bead embroidery stitches.

Size 6° and 10° triangular beads

Triangular beads have three sides and come in sizes 6° to 15°. These beads can be used for the bead embroidery and bead woven stitches.

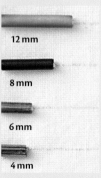

Size 12 mm, 8 mm, 6 mm, and 4 mm bugle beads

Bugle beads are long and cylindrical in shape, often with faceted sides, and come in sizes 2 mm to 20 mm. These beads can be worked into several of the bead embroidery stitches.

Not All Beads Are Created Equal ...

1. 6° seed bead
2. 8° seed bead
3. 11° seed bead
4. 8° seed bead
5. 7 mm bugle bead
6. 11° seed bead
7. 11° seed bead
8. 8° seed bead
9. 11° seed bead
10. 15° seed bead
11. 6° seed bead
12. 11° seed bead
13. 4° square bead
14. 8° seed bead
15. 11° seed bead

Most of the glass beads that you find today (sold loose in packages or in tubes by weight) are made in Japan and are, for the most part, even in size and shape. The consistency in size and shape make them an excellent choice for both bead woven and bead embroidery stitches. See 7 in the bead sampler (at right).

Beads made in the Czech Republic (usually sold in hanks of 10–14 strands, in 14"–20" lengths per strand) may differ slightly in size. The slight imperfections in size and shape are not a problem for most bead embroidery stitches but lend a challenge to bead woven stitches. See 6 in the bead sampler (at right).

Examples of a bead woven flower: **A.** Evenly shaped beads, **B.** Unevenly shaped beads

❋ Tip: Bead Blips

In your group of beads, you will occasionally find a "bead blip": a bead that is not quite formed or that doesn't have a hole. I put these into a glass jar and just look at them to appreciate the colors.

Bead sampler

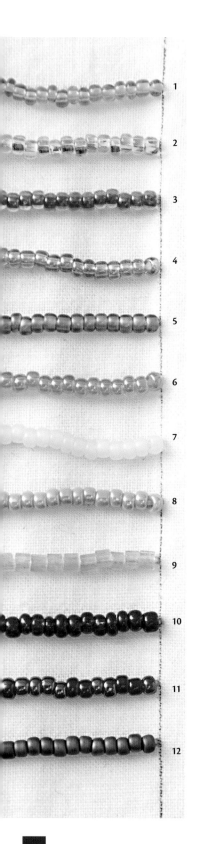

Finishes

Glass beads are made from sand; the colors are achieved by adding various materials. Once the bead is made, additional effects can be created by adding color to the surface of the bead or to the inside of the bead hole.

1. Transparent: Clear color with a shiny finish

2. Gold or silver lined: Transparent color with gold or silver painted inside the bead hole

3. Color lined: Transparent color with a different color painted inside the bead hole

4. Aurora borealis (AB): Transparent color with an AB (pink, green, and gold) finish

5. Matte AB: Transparent color with a matte AB (pink, green, and gold) finish

6. Luster: Transparent color with a gold-washed finish

7. Opaque: Solid color with a flat nonreflective finish

8. Opaque lustered: Solid color with a shiny finish

9. Ceylon: Solid color with a shiny whitish finish

10. Metallic: Heavy solid metallic finish

11. Iris: Matte *or* shiny multicolored hues of purple, blue, green, or gunmetal

12. Raku: Matte with multiple hues

EMBELLISHMENTS GALORE: THE MORE THE MERRIER!

Adding larger beads, charms, and buttons gives interest and definition to your project. The beads and charms are measured by millimeters: the lower the number, the smaller the bead. Buttons are measured in lines or fractions of an inch. The materials vary, so keep in mind the weight of these items, prepare your base, and place them accordingly.

Large Beads, Sequins, Charms, and Buttons

Glass beads

Rondelles

Sequins

Metal charms

Flower, leaf, and motif charms

Buttons

Larger **glass beads** can be round, oblong, or square. They come in sizes 2 mm to 20 mm.

Rondelles are flat or puffed, circular or floral shaped with a single hole in the center. They come in sizes 4 mm and larger. These can be made from glass, shell, metal, or plastic.

Sequins are round or square with a center hole and are made from Mylar or nylon. Novelty shapes have a hole in the center or as a part of the design.

Metal charms come with a hole that is part of the design. The position of the hole determines how it will be sewn to the project. Various metal and metal alloys are used.

Flower, leaf, and motif shaped charms come with a hole that is part of the design. The position of the hole determines how it will be sewn to the project. These can be made from glass, shell, or plastic.

Buttons come in two styles, sew on or shank. Sew-on buttons have two to four holes through the middle of the face. Shank buttons have a solid face; the back of the button has a small section with a hole in it or a metal loop. Buttons can be made from glass, shell, wood, metal, or plastic.

USING COLOR EFFECTIVELY

The coloring of the bead can also make a difference and a great deal of impact on a design. For instance, the coloring of a clear bead remains the same whether the side of the bead is positioned flat against the fabric or turned to see the hole. A lined bead, however, changes in color. When positioned flat against the fabric, you see the combination of both colors, but when turned to see the hole, you see the lining color. Beads that are made with a variety of colors or finishes, like an aurora borealis finish, vary per bead and offer another design element.

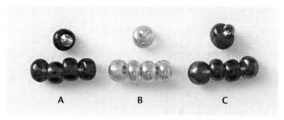

A. Clear and solid-color beads, B. Lined beads, C. Aurora borealis (AB) and multi-finished beads

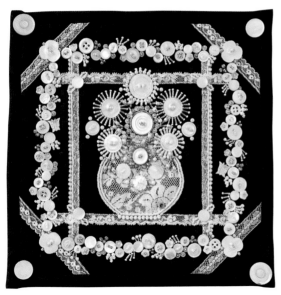

Champagne and Pearls (page 154), gallery inspiration for Feminine Fancies project (page 86)

Welcome Home (page 154), gallery inspiration for Feminine Fancies project (page 86)

Here are two examples of the same design worked with different fabrics, beads, and button shapes. The first example with the black background is quite striking. The embroidery is worked in an almost monochromatic color scheme using solid-color beads. The second example uses color in a different way: It starts with a solid and a printed fabric, and the beads and embellishments are in a variety of colors and finishes.

INTRODUCTION TO BEADING TECHNIQUES

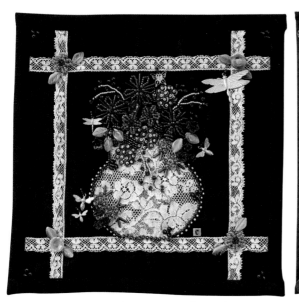

Feminine Fancies: Bouquet of Flowers project (page 88)

Eastern Influences (page 155)

The use of beads in the bead embroidery and bead woven stitches bring a surprisingly visual and dimensional aspect to your work. The projects and gallery examples in this book also include other components, such as buttons, ribbonwork flowers, trims, and found objects.

For more information, see Beads and Embellishments: Candy with No Calories! (page 17) for bead sizes, shapes, and colors; Let's Get Started! (page 36) for tools, needle sizes, and other tips; and Bead Embroidery and Bead Woven Stitches (page 45) for instructions.

STITCHES: TRADITIONAL TO CONTEMPORARY

Many forms of thread embroidery can be adapted to bead embroidery and bead woven stitches. In Bead Embroidery and Bead Woven Stitches (page 45), you will find both traditional bead embroidery stitches and unique techniques that accommodate the special characteristics of the different bead shapes and sizes.

Crazy-pieced etui using perle cotton, floss, and silk embroidery ribbon

Detail of CQ Sewing Caddy: Ivory and Pastel project (see full photo and project instructions, page 132), using a variety of bead shapes and sizes

Crazy- and strip-pieced projects use a variety of traditional and silk ribbon embroidery stitches to embellish seams and open spaces.

Sashiko embroidery is a very stylistic embroidery, worked with a straight or running stitch using a sashiko cotton thread.

A. Thread example of sashiko pattern worked in perle cotton,
B. Bead example worked with size 11° seed beads

Cross stitch embroidery is worked with the cross stitch in a pattern. It can be a simple outline or a shape that is entirely filled in with stitches.

A. Thread example of cross stitch worked in perle cotton #8,
B. Bead example worked in size 11° seed beads

Brazilian embroidery stitches are worked in textured and raised stitches that rest above the fabric's surface.

A. Thread example of Brazilian embroidery worked in perle cotton,
B. Bead example worked with size 11° and 15° seed beads (See Brazilian Roses, project inspiration for Beaded Brooches, page 94.)

BEAD EMBROIDERY

CQ Sewing Caddy: Ivory and Pastel project (page 132)

(page 132)

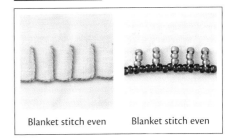

BORDER ROW

Blanket stitch even   Blanket stitch even

FLOWERS

Lazy daisy
stitch flower   Flower with lazy
daisy petals

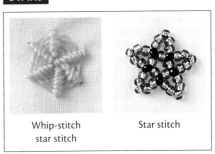

STARS

Whip-stitch
star stitch   Star stitch

Thread and Bead Embroidery Comparisons

Bead embroidery is a technique where the beads are stitched onto a piece of fabric using a special beading thread and needle to form a design, a border row, or an individual stitch.

In thread embroidery, when forming a looped stitch such as the feather stitch, the thread comes out of the cup of the stitch to catch that stitch and begin the next one.

In bead embroidery, the needle can be stitched inside the cup to catch the stitch; then beads that will be used to form the next stitch are added.

Another option is to stitch the needle through a bead in the middle of the cup to catch the stitch and then add the beads that will be used to form the next stitch.

Continuous Stitch Rows

Continuous stitches are worked with the beads forming a line or row of stitches. These rows can be worked along a seam, shape, or imaginary line.

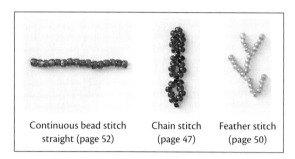

| Continuous bead stitch straight (page 52) | Chain stitch (page 47) | Feather stitch (page 50) |

Individual Stitches

Individual stitches are created with one bead or several beads to create a single unit. These stitches can be a decorative or detail stitch, or they can be used to create a border row of beaded stitches.

DECORATIVE STITCHES

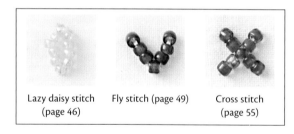

| Lazy daisy stitch (page 46) | Fly stitch (page 49) | Cross stitch (page 55) |

DETAIL STITCHES

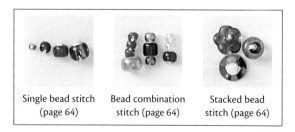

| Single bead stitch (page 64) | Bead combination stitch (page 64) | Stacked bead stitch (page 64) |

Combined Stitches

A single stitch can be grouped and repeated to create a shape or larger component. A composite stitch is comprised of one or more individual stitches worked to create a larger component.

GROUPED STITCHES

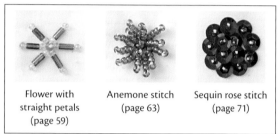

| Flower with straight petals (page 59) | Anemone stitch (page 63) | Sequin rose stitch (page 71) |

COMPOSITE STITCHES

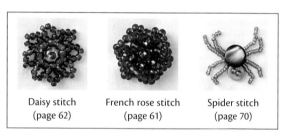

| Daisy stitch (page 62) | French rose stitch (page 61) | Spider stitch (page 70) |

Beaded Shapes

These stitches are worked directly onto the fabric to create a realistic shape.

| Knot stitch (page 62) | Hippie flower stitch (page 62) | Snail stitch (page 63) |

Embellishments

Buttons, sequins, and glass or metal charms can be added to any project.

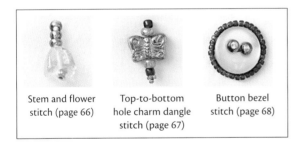

| Stem and flower stitch (page 66) | Top-to-bottom hole charm dangle stitch (page 67) | Button bezel stitch (page 68) |

BEADED EDGES

Beaded edges are worked around a ribbon rosette, fabric yo-yo, or a finished edge, such as in the Beaded Brooches project (page 94). A beaded edge is also used to stitch together the two layers of ribbon in Beaded Bracelets (page 108).

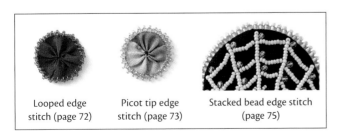

| Looped edge stitch (page 72) | Picot tip edge stitch (page 73) | Stacked bead edge stitch (page 75) |

Midnight Serenade Brooch (page 148)

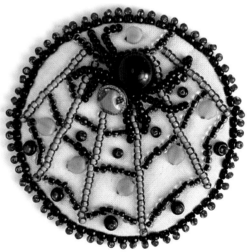

Spooky Spider Brooch (page 147)

BEAD WOVEN STITCHES

Beaded Bracelets: The Stars Are Out Tonight project (page 112)

Bead woven stitches, such as the peyote, net, and brick stitches, are formed independently from the fabric and are considered more like individual charms. The advantage is that realistic shapes can be made without pulling or distorting the fabric base. These shapes are then attached to the fabric using the beginning and end lengths of the thread that was used to create the stitch.

Even Peyote and Free-Form Peyote Stitches

Traditionally, the even peyote and free-form peyote stitches are worked into a shape or form, independent of the fabric. However, the stitch can be worked off of a row of the continuous bead stitch (page 52) that is worked directly onto a fabric base.

Even peyote stitch row (page 78)

Free-form peyote stitch row (page 79)

The even peyote stitch begins with a row of beads. The following rows are worked through a bead in the previous row, adding one bead, then skipping a bead in the row, and so on.

Row 1
Row 2

Even peyote stitch

The free-form peyote stitch is a less rigid technique than the even peyote stitch. One difference is that you can use different shapes and sizes of beads within the row. Another difference is that you can add one or more beads per stitch into the previous row.

Row 1
Row 2

Free-form peyote stitch

This is a work in process, showing an example of how the free-form peyote stitch can be transformed into an organic shape using a variety of bead shapes and sizes.

Circular Peyote and Netted Stitches

The circular peyote stitch is worked in complete rows that increase in size by adding one or more beads into a bead in the previous row to create the shape.

Circular peyote stitch

A netted stitch can be worked in a straight row, like the peyote stitch, or in a circular row, like the circular peyote stitch. The difference is that more beads are added in the following rows, skipping several beads in the previous row to create a shape or netted design.

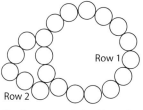

Circular peyote stitch with netting

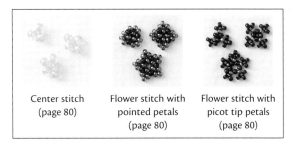

| Center stitch (page 80) | Flower stitch with pointed petals (page 80) | Flower stitch with picot tip petals (page 80) |

| Starfish stitch (page 81) | Double flower stitch (page 81) | Spider webbed stitch (page 82) |

Brick Stitches

The brick stitch is worked in horizontal rows, with the beads stitched side by side in the row. The following rows are worked with an increase or decrease of beads.

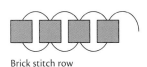

Brick stitch row

| Basket stitch (page 83) | Simple leaf stitch (page 84) | Pointed leaf stitch (page 84) |

WHERE DO DESIGNS COME FROM?

INSPIRATION

The Shore, project inspiration for Beaded Bracelets (page 108)

Millefiori Flower Basket, project inspiration for Beaded Brooches (page 94), with millefiori earrings

Inspiration for a design can come from nature and your surroundings. I frequently use real-life images such as flowers, shells, stars, and spiderwebs in my work. The colors, shapes, and sizes of an image can be manipulated to fit your design and the colors that you have chosen for the project.

Cogs and Gears with printed felt, project inspiration for Blowing Bubbles (page 121)

A fabric with a strong print can also be used as the focal or base of an embroidered design. The embroidery and embellishments can follow the lines and shapes of the print and enhance any open spaces.

Any type of consistent dimensional or realistic design can be adapted to bead embroidery and bead woven stitches. An example is the millefiori mosaic work, where multicolored glass canes are cut crosswise into small thin sections to form a pattern of flowers or other designs.

See Beads and Embellishments: Candy with No Calories! (page 17) for bead sizes and finishes, Introduction to Beading Techniques (page 23) for stitch definitions, and Bead Embroidery and Bead Woven Stitches (page 45) for instructions.

Special Note

My motto is this: If you are going to do it, make it show! The more you put into the work, the more meaningful and grander the overall project will be. Have fun with this! Make sure to give yourself time to work—a few hours at least—so you can concentrate on learning the stitches and getting comfortable with the techniques.

DESIGN PROCESS

Wild Persimmons (page 156)

Each project has a story to tell. The creation can begin simply with a wonderful piece of fabric or a special embellishment such as a button or charm. While gathering the components for each project, I begin with a key set of elements that help tell the story.

COLOR SWATCH CHART

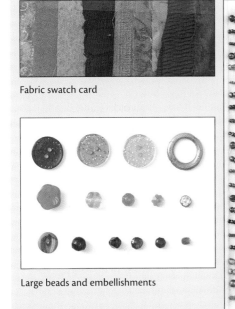

Fabric swatch card

Large beads and embellishments

Bead sample

Theme: The theme may start with the colors, the construction, or the embroidery components. In this case, it was the wild, wonderful colors of the fabric: persimmon, magenta, tangerine, fuchsia, and more.

Color: The colors of the pallet can be traditional, subtle, or complex. In this case, I chose bold, warm floral tones and included bronze and copper accents.

Fabric: The fabric itself is important, but it should not overpower the components and embroidery designs. Here, I used both cotton and silk fabrics and both solid and printed fabrics, along with lace, rayon ribbon, and rattail cord.

Construction: A wholecloth background provides an open canvas for the embroidery design; a pieced background provides lines for the embroidery design to follow. In this case, I only had small amounts of fabric to work with, so I made a crazy-pieced base, which was then machine quilted.

Embroidery design: The embroidery design is determined by the fabric and construction of the background and the components gathered for embroidery and embellishment. The embroidery design here is worked around the rayon cord, which I first couched down in an organic spiral design.

Embroidery materials and embellishments: Choose beads, buttons, and other components in a variety of shapes and sizes with colors that complement the fabrics. I used a large vintage button for the main focal point and then added additional plastic and glass buttons; ribbon rosettes were spaced between the buttons. The beading is worked around these components.

CHOOSING A PROJECT

Included in Project Designs (page 85) are eight projects, with some having two or more designs to choose from. Each has its own unique characteristics, style, skill level, and, of course, commitment.

In most cases, I included additional examples of the project for inspiration. These may be worked in a different colorway of fabrics, beads, and embellishments. In some instances, the inspirational piece has a different skill level or take on the design.

Feminine Fancies (page 86)

This project offers two appliqué designs: a fan and a vase, both of which are worked on a wholecloth background. Each design is worked with a different pattern of bead embroidery and embellishments. This project requires a sewing machine, and each project takes a few days to complete.

Beaded Brooches (page 94)

This project begins with a solid-color base of fabric, which is stitched to form around a firm stabilizer. The base is then embroidered and embellished with beads. This project is all hand-sewn; each design is a little different in technique and skill level.

Project A: *Bouquet of Flowers*, bead embroidery and bead woven stitches; skill level: intermediate to advanced

Project B: *Fan and Flowers*, bead embroidery stitches; skill level: intermediate to advanced

Project B: Ash Tree, bead embroidery and bead woven stitches; skill level: intermediate

Project A: Spring in Bloom, bead embroidery stitches; skill level: beginner

Spider's Webs (page 102)

This project begins with a wholecloth base that is machine quilted. The base is then stitched to a firm stabilizer, and the pattern is worked with bead embroidery stitches. This project requires a sewing machine. The skill level required is intermediate; the project takes a dedicated week to complete.

Beaded Bracelets (page 108)

This project begins with a length of grosgrain ribbon, embellished with a narrower ribbon or piece of lace. The base is then embroidered with beads, buttons, and charms, using a variety of stitches and techniques. This project is all hand-sewn; each design is a little different in technique and skill level.

Project A: Summer Blooms, ribbonwork rosette with bead embroidery stitches; skill level: beginner to intermediate

Project B: The Stars Are Out Tonight, bead woven and bead embroidery stitches; skill level: intermediate to advanced

Project: *Spiders Hide in the Dusk*, bead embroidery stitches

Inspiration: *Along Came a Spider*, free-form peyote stitch, bead embroidery and bead woven stitches; skill level: intermediate to advanced

Scrap Roll (page 114)

This project begins with a ribbon base that is collaged with bits of lace, fabric, ribbons, and trims. The collage is then embellished with appliqués, fabric yo-yos, ribbon rosettes, bead embroidery, buttons, and charms. This project is all hand-sewn with bead embroidery and bead woven stitches. The skill level required is intermediate to advanced; the project takes a dedicated week to complete.

Project: Ivory and Lace, bead embroidery and bead woven stitches

Inspiration: Pansies and Sunflowers, bead embroidery stitches

Blowing Bubbles (page 121)

This project begins with a reverse appliqué technique using solid and printed felt squares. The top layer has several circles randomly cut out; the bottom layers are then overlapped behind. The bead embroidery and embellishments follow the circle shapes and open spaces. This project is all hand-sewn. The skill level required is intermediate; the project takes a few days to complete.

Project: Jewel Bubbles, bead embroidery

Inspiration: *Cogs and Gears*, bead embroidery

Beaded Tandletons (page 126)

This project begins with a length of silk bias ribbon that is cut and stitched into a little stuffed pillow shape. The beads are then embroidered onto the pillow shape using a variety of decorative and detail stitches. This project is all hand-sewn with bead embroidery and bead woven stitches. One pillow shape can be stitched and embroidered in a few hours; the skill level required is beginner to intermediate.

Miss Muffet, her Pretty Maids, and her Fair Misses are made from a variety of ribbon widths with bead embroidery and bead woven stitches.
Project A: Miss Muffet, 2½" silk satin bias ribbon
Project B: Pretty Maids, 1½" silk habotai bias ribbon
Project C: Fair Misses, 1" silk habotai bias ribbon

CQ Sewing Caddy (page 132)

This project starts with five or six pieces of fabric cut into strips and wedge shapes, which are crazy pieced onto a muslin foundation. The bead embroidery and other embellishments follow the pieced lines and open areas of fabric. This project requires a sewing machine. The skill level required is intermediate to advanced; the project takes a dedicated week to complete.

Project: Ivory and Pastel, bead embroidery and bead woven stitches

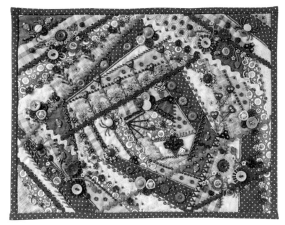

Inspiration: *Primarily Crazy for Kevin*, bead embroidery

LET'S GET STARTED!

1. Cotton fabrics and trims; **2.** Felt; **3.** Batik fabric and trim; **4.** Linen fabric, lace yardage, and lace trims; **5.** Hankies, wide ribbon, lace and trims, and appliqués; **6.** Hanah Silk bias ribbons; **7.** Grosgrain ribbons

CHOOSING YOUR PALETTE

The fabrics, trims, beads, and embellishments that you choose should reflect the type of project you are making. Begin by choosing the base fabric(s) or ribbon; then, for additional design options, add in laces, ribbons, trims, and cords. When gathering beads and embellishments, choose colors and finishes that complement your other components.

See Beads and Embellishments: Candy with No Calories! (page 17) for bead and embellishments ideas. See Where Do Designs Come From? (page 30) for further information about the projects in this book.

GATHERING THE GOODS

Cotton, denim, linen, moiré, and silk are all suitable fabrics for many of the projects included in this book. Choose solid colors, subtle cotton prints, or abstract designs, such as batiks or dyed fabrics.

Ribbons, lace, appliqués, trims, and cords can be used to create a design or focal point on the base fabric. These can be machine or hand stitched to the background and used as part of the design or to complete the edge of a project.

Choose the beads, buttons, and other embellishments to complement the fabrics, ribbons, and trims you are working with. Choose as many color groups as you have for your fabric, adding in additional colors as needed. If you are working with a solid-color base, use as many color groups as you want.

Specific Materials

- **Felt squares:** Either synthetic, wool, or wool blend
- **Lace yardage and flat lace trims**
- **Hanah Silk bias ribbon and grosgrain ribbon**

How Much Do I Need?

There is something to be said about having a well-stocked creative stash. These materials don't go bad, and you never know what you might need! That being said, all the projects I designed for this book require very little in the way of materials (see each project for specific amounts). In general, here are a few guidelines.

- **Fabric:** Small amounts, such as fat quarters, are enough for a base; however, a ½ yard or more may be required for the lining and binding in some projects.

- **Lace fabric and appliqués:** ¼ yard of lace fabric and 2–10 appliqués; the amount depends on the design of the project.

- **Ribbon, lace, trim, and cord yardage:** 1- to 3-yard lengths should be sufficient; the amount depends on the design of the project.

- **Perle cotton #8:** 1 color

- **Beads:** 1 package of size 11°, 8°, and/or 6° seed beads in each color group; 1 package of size 15° in 1 or 2 colors (though it is unlikely that you will use the entire package on one project). Larger beads, buttons, and other embellishments depend on the design of the project.

Tip: Organizing Materials

I keep the beginning components of each project in a box or bag, adding additional items as I find them. To keep myself organized, I make a swatch card (see, for example, the *Wild Persimmons* Color Swatch Chart, page 31) of my chosen fabrics for the project. This is useful when shopping for additional fabrics, beads, and other materials. I do the same for the seed beads. I then put the larger components in a plastic bag.

GENERAL SEWING INFORMATION

Tools for Sewing

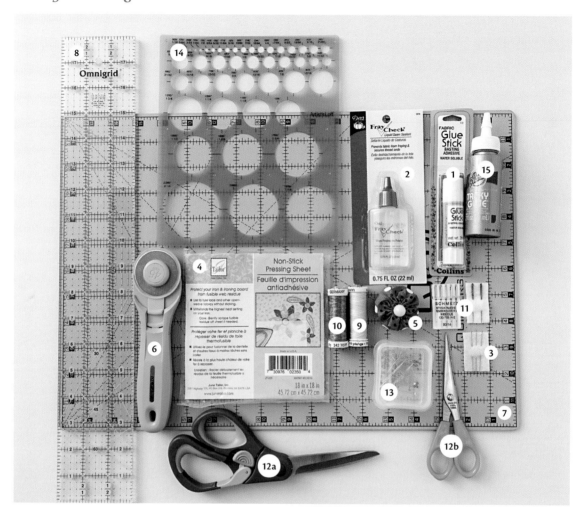

1. Fabric glue stick

2. Fray Check (to prevent fabric or lace edges from fraying)

3. Needles, small sharps

4. Nonstick pressing sheet

5. Pincushion

6. Rotary cutter

7. Rotary mat

8. Quilter's acrylic ruler

9. Sewing thread (to match the project)

10. Topstitching thread for project

11. Sewing machine needles: Regular and topstitch

12. Scissors:

  a. Fabric

  b. Craft

13. Straight pins

14. Stencils, circle shapes

15. Tacky glue, such as Aleene's Original Tacky Glue (to attach small fiber items)

16. Sulky KK 2000 Temporary Spray Adhesive (*not pictured*)

17. Chalk pencil (*not pictured*)

The Foundation

Each project in this book requires some form of stabilizer, which is used to keep the base firm and wrinkle free and to eliminate the need for an embroidery hoop. The stabilizer also helps the fabric maintain its shape from the weight of the beads and the embellishments. When working with any stabilizer, be sure to follow the manufacturer's instructions.

STABILIZERS

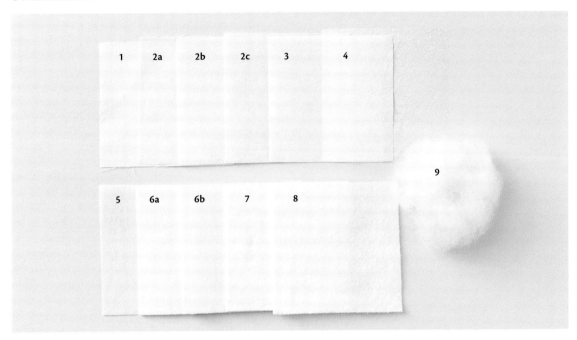

1. 100% cotton muslin is used for foundation piecing on strip- and crazy-pieced bases.

2. Interfacings, such as Pellon fusible interfacing, create a firm background and stabilize the fabric base:

  a. Sheerweight

  b. Featherweight

  c. Midweight

3. HeatnBond Lite is used to fuse one fabric to another.

4. Mistyfuse is used to fuse a piece of lace to fabric.

5. Pellon 809 Décor-Bond is used for projects that need a thin, firm stability to hold the shape of a project.

6. fast2fuse (by C&T Publishing) is a double-sided fusible interfacing that comes in light-, medium-, and heavyweight versions. I used the medium weight in the projects that have fast2fuse. It gives stability and holds the shape of a project:

  a. Light

  b. Heavy

7. Timtex (by C&T Publishing) gives stability and holds the shape of a project.

8. Warm & Natural cotton batting (craft size) gives the fabric base a firm but softer dimension. It can also be added to create a padded look to the project.

9. Polyfill stuffing gives dimension to a form such as a pillow or Tandleton.

Fabric Preparation and Sewing Tips

- Prewash all fabrics before you begin cutting, piecing, or stitching. This eliminates the sizing, prevents colors from bleeding, and prevents further shrinkage if the item will be washed.

- To keep the fabric pieces in a collage base in place while pinning or stitching, I recommend using Sulky KK 2000 Temporary Spray Adhesive. For smaller pieces of ribbon or lace, use a fabric glue stick.

- For a project that has a pieced base, use a ¼″ seam allowance (unless otherwise noted).

- Be sure not to backstitch at the beginning or end of a pieced seam (unless otherwise noted), as this adds bulk to the fabric base.

- When using a fusible stabilizer, follow the manufacturer's instructions and fuse it onto the wrong side of the fabric foundation *after* all the piecing is completed.

- To avoid frayed edges, I recommend you serge or zigzag the outer raw edges of the fabric base before you work the stitches. To help prevent further fraying, you can apply a thin line of Fray Check on the raw edges, following the manufacturer's instructions.

- When stitching by hand, use the thread single. Thread a small sharps needle with sewing thread or a cotton darner with perle cotton and knot the tail.

Decorative Machine-Stitched Backgrounds

I like to add a layer of machine stitching to both wholecloth and pieced projects that are backed with batting. This adds an additional design element while preventing the batting from traveling or distorting.

FREE-FORM STITCHING

1. Cut the batting 2″ larger than the fabric. Place the batting on the wrong side of the fabric; pin through the fabric to hold the layers in place.

2. Thread the sewing machine with decorative top-stitching thread; if you use a metallic thread, use a lightweight thread in the bobbin. Set the stitch length to a top-stitch length.

3. Begin in the center of the square at the raw edge. Stitch down the length in either a straight or a curved line; finish at the opposite raw edge.

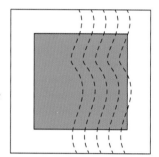

4. Turn the fabric in the machine and continue to stitch about ½″ away from the previous line.

5. Continue to stitch this half of the square. Repeat for the other half.

STITCHED SEAMS

1. For a pieced base, cut the piece of batting 1″ larger than the pieced fabric.

2. Follow Steps 1 and 2 of Free-Form Stitching (above).

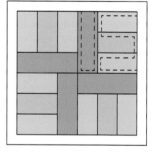

3. Begin at a raw edge next to a seam. Stitch ⅛″ from the seam.

4. *Continue stitching around the next seam and so on. Backstitch and start; repeat from * when needed.

BEAD EMBROIDERY BASICS

Tools for Embroidery

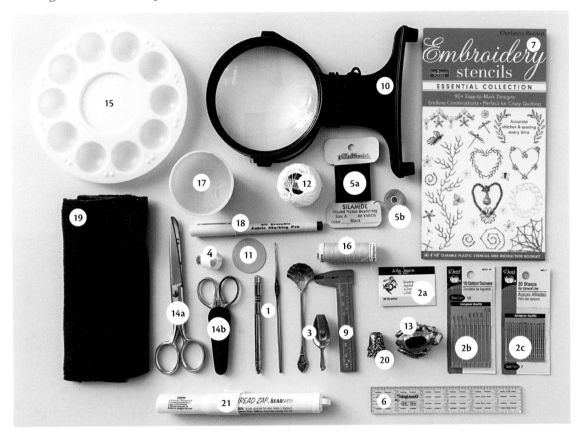

1. Small crochet hook or awl, used to take knots out of beading thread

2. Needles:

    a. Beading, long and short

    b. Cotton darners for perle cotton

    c. Small sharps for sewing thread

3. Bead scoop or teaspoon to pick up loose beads

4. Bead thimble to pick up beads and thread onto needle

5. Bead threads:

    a. Silamide size A: a two-ply thread made of waxed nylon that comes on a card

    b. Nymo size B: a flat, supple nylon thread that comes on a small bobbin

6. 6″ clear quilter's ruler

7. fast2mark Embroidery Stencils, Essential Collection (by C&T Publishing)

8. Full-spectrum light (*not pictured*)

9. Gauge to measure larger beads and components

10. Magnifier to see those tiny treasures

11. Needle gripper to pull the needle through the layers of fabric

12. Perle cotton to sew buttons, trim, or edges

13. Pincushion

14. Scissors:

    a. Fabric

    b. Embroidery

15. Segmented bead dish or plastic painter's palette

16. Sewing thread to match fabric or ribbon

17. Synthetic beeswax to condition the beading thread

18. Air-erasable pen, such as The Fine Line air-erasable marking pen, to mark embroidery lines (**Note:** *Follow the manufacturer's instructions.*)

19. Thermal bead mat to keep beads from sliding around work surface

20. Thimble

21. Thread Zap II pen to fuse the raw edges of woven ribbons

THREAD AND NEEDLE SPECIFICS

Beading threads are used to stitch the beads. When used for bead embroidery, the thread is used double with a knotted tail. When used for bead woven stitches, the thread is used single unless otherwise noted. Choose a color that is neutral to the fabric, beads, and embellishments. Start with a 3-yard length for embroidery and a 1-yard length for bead weaving.

Beading needles are fine and thin and are most commonly found in sizes 10–13. I prefer the John James brand of needles. They come in both a short and a long length. I prefer to use the long needles for both bead embroidery and bead weaving, but I find that most people choose what works for them.

THREADING THE NEEDLE AND WAXING

1. Cut the end of the thread so that it is straight across.

2. Hold the end of the thread close to the eye of the needle and insert the thread 1″ or so beyond the eye.

For a single thread, follow Step 3.

If you are working with the thread doubled, fold the length in half, with the middle of the thread at the eye of the needle. Match the tails together and follow Steps 3–5.

3. Place the eye of the needle next to the wax; pull the thread firmly over the wax.

4. Place the eye of the needle at your forefinger and close your thumb over the thread. Pull the thread through your fingers to merge the 2 threads.

5. Knot the ends together.

WAXING TIPS

- If the thread does not stay together after the first pass through the wax, then wax the thread again.

- When removing the thread from the needle, cut the thread close to the eye; then pull the short thread out of the eye. This prevents a wax buildup in the eye of the needle.

- The goal of waxing the thread is to keep the two threads together but not to have so much wax that you have clumps in the thread that will end up on the fabric. You can brush a soft, new toothbrush across the surface of the beads to remove unwanted wax buildup on the fabric's surface.

KNOTTING AND FINISHING THE THREAD

1. Anchor the thread on the wrong side of the fabric with a knot into the fabric.

2. Stitch the needle to the right side of the stitched pattern piece.

3. Follow the directions for the stitch.

4. Knot the end of the thread on the wrong side of the fabric.

EMBROIDERY FROM START TO FINISH

Getting Organized

I place all my tools and supplies on the thermal bead mat, which I place on a TV tray so that I can easily move it.

I put a teaspoon scoop of each bead, arranged by color and size, onto the thermal mat. This way, I can see the beads within the color groups. Note that, in most cases, you need only a portion of seed beads suggested in the supply list for each project.

Make sure that you have a good light source by your worktable.

METHODS FOR PICKING UP THE BEADS

After laying out a group of beads onto a mat, use one of the following methods:

Bead thimble: Push the sticky side into the beads to pick up a group. Thread the desired number of beads onto the needle.

Peck and scoop: Push the needle toward a bead with an exposed hole and scoop up the bead.

Pick up and thread: Pick up a group of beads on the finger of one hand and place them directly onto the needle with the other hand.

Where to Embroider

It is always a good idea to practice a new stitch before you work on a project. I suggest using a piece of cotton muslin backed with featherweight interfacing (such as Pellon featherweight interfacing) as the base for bead embroidered stitches.

When following the directions and illustrations of a stitch, it is important to follow the number and position of the beads; otherwise, the stitch will not be formed correctly.

When working any single or grouped stitch, knot when the directions call for it, but do not cut the thread until the design is complete.

SEAMS

Embroider over the seam or next to the seam—that is entirely up to you.

Work the seams descending in order from long to short, from the beginning to the end of the row.

Remember the seam allowance! Don't stitch beyond ¾" from the raw edge of the seam; otherwise, you may damage the sewing machine needle or break the bead during the assembly process.

SHAPES

Transfer the design with an air-erasable pen. For long lines such as spiderwebs, draw in the length of the shape. For small flowers, transfer the center of the flower and then the points for the petals.

Individual stitches can be worked following the design or pattern alone or in groups.

Follow the directions for the bead woven stitches, working the stitch as directed. Start with a 1-yard length of thread since you will not be able to add thread during the stitch.

Each bead woven component begins and ends with a 6" tail. These tails are used to attach the component to the fabric. The tails are knotted to the wrong side of the fabric.

Keep in mind that some of the stitches may have an extra detail that will be stitched between the sections of the stitch.

THREAD CHALLENGES

If you need to add thread to complete an embroidered stitch, end the thread at a point where the needle is on the wrong side of the fabric. Knot and cut the thread.

At some point, you may have to remove the thread from a row of beads or remove or "un-stitch" the thread from the fabric. No worries—it happens to the best of us!

 *Tip: Un-stitching*

To remove the needle from the fabric, hold onto the needle with one hand and pull the thread from behind; the needle will follow the path of the thread. Slightly tug the thread when the eye of the needle meets the fabric, and it should pull right through.

To remove the needle from a stitch, insert a knotting awl or crochet hook into the loop of thread next to the bead; then pull the thread out of the row of beads with the needle dangling behind. The needle will follow the path of the thread.

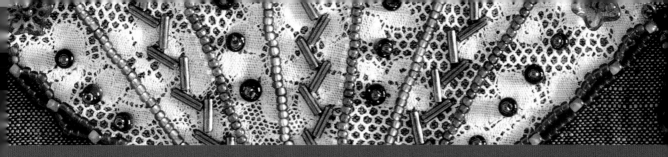

BEAD EMBROIDERY AND BEAD WOVEN STITCHES

BEAD EMBROIDERY STITCHES

Spider's Webs: *Spiders Hide in the Dusk* project (page 102)

Feminine Fancies: *Fan and Flowers* project (page 91)

In bead embroidery, the beads are stitched onto the fabric using a special beading needle and thread. The stitches form a design, a border row, or an individual stitch. In this section, you will see beads translated into traditional embroidery stitches, as well as some unique techniques that use larger beads, buttons, sequins, and charms.

The letters included in the illustrations indicate where the hole of the bead is and where the needle should come up or go down through the fabric.

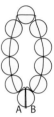

To create a looped stitch, pass the needle through the first bead added, in the opposite direction to finish the loop.

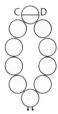

To finish a looped stitch, pass the needle through the middle bead in the row.

NEEDLE AND THREAD SPECIFICS

For the following embroidery stitches, cut 3-yard lengths of beading thread; then thread the needle, double the thread, wax, and knot the tails.

Refer to the following chapters for further information:

- Introduction to Beading Techniques (page 23) for detailed explanations
- Where Do Designs Come From? (page 30) for ideas and project information
- Project Designs (page 85)
- Let's Get Started! (page 36) for tools and tips

LAZY DAISY AND CHAIN STITCHES

Lazy Daisy Stitch

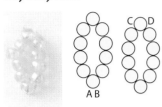

1. Come up at **A**. Thread 10 size 11° seed beads onto the needle. Lay the beads flat against the fabric. Take the needle back through the first bead. Go down at **B**. Knot the thread.

2. Come up at **C**, stitch through the middle bead, and go down at **D**. Knot the thread.

Note: *To make a longer stitch, increase the number of beads by 4.*

Lazy Daisy Stitch Loose

Follow Step 1 of the lazy daisy stitch (at left), but do not lay the beads flat against fabric.

Lazy Daisy Stitch Fancy

1. Come up at **A**. Thread 1 size 8° and 11 size 11° seed beads onto the needle. Lay the beads flat against the fabric. Take the needle back through the size 8° bead. Go down at **B**. Knot the thread.

2. Come up at **C**, stitch through the middle bead, and go down at **D**. Knot the thread.

Note: *To make a longer stitch, increase the number of size 11° beads by 4.*

Lazy Daisy Stitch with Loop

1. Follow Step 1 of the lazy daisy stitch (above) with 11 size 11° seed beads.

2. Come up at **C**. Thread 5 size 11° seed beads onto the needle and pass them down to the fabric.

3. Go down at **D**. Knot the thread.

Note: *To make a longer stitch, increase the number of beads in Step 1 by 4. The loop can also be made with 7 size 15° seed beads.*

Lazy Daisy Stitch with Tip

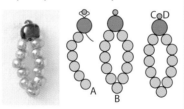

1. Come up at **A**. Thread 6 size 11°, 1 size 8°, and 1 size 15° seed beads onto the needle. Lay the beads flat against the fabric. Take the needle back through the size 8° bead.

2. Thread 5 size 11° seed beads onto the needle and lay them flat against fabric. Take the needle back through the first bead. Go down at **B**. Knot the thread.

3. Come up at **C**, stitch through the middle bead, and go down at **D**. Knot the thread.

Lazy Daisy Stitch with Tail

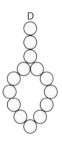

1. Follow Step 1 of the lazy daisy stitch (above left) with 11 size 11° seed beads.

2. Come up at **C**. Thread 3 size 11° seed beads onto the needle and pass them down to the fabric.

3. Lay the thread between the fifth and sixth beads in the stitch. Go down at **D**. Knot the thread.

Note: *To make a longer stitch, increase the number of beads in Step 1 by 4. The loop can also be made with 7 size 15° seed beads.*

Lazy Daisy Stitch with Center

A B

C D

1. Center: Come up and thread 3 size 11° seed beads onto the needle. Go down past the last bead. Knot the thread.

2. Loop: Come up at **A**. Thread 12 size 11° seed beads onto the needle and lay the beads flat against the fabric with the loop formed around the center. Take the needle back through the first bead. Go down at **B**. Knot the thread.

3. Come up at **C**, stitch through the middle bead, and go down at **D**. Knot the thread.

Note: To make a longer stitch, increase the number of beads in Step 1 by 2 and in Step 2 by 4. The center can also be a bugle bead; adjust the beads in Step 2 to fit.

Lazy Daisy Stitch Border Rows

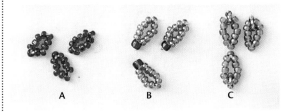

A B C

A. Zigzag, **B.** V shape, **C.** Split spaced

Follow the directions for any of the lazy daisy stitches (previous page and this page), working the stitches along a seam or drawn line.

Chain Stitch

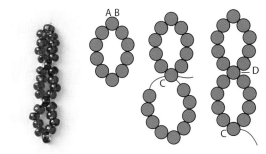

A B

C

D

C

1. Come up at **A**. Thread 10 size 11° seed beads onto the needle and lay the beads flat against the fabric. Take the needle back through the first bead. Go down at **B**. Knot the thread.

2. *Come up at **C** and stitch through the middle bead of the previous loop. Thread 9 size 11° seed beads onto the needle and lay the beads flat against the fabric. Stitch through the middle bead again and down through the fabric at **D**. Knot the thread.

3. To finish the row, continue from * through the middle bead of the previous loop.

Note: To make a longer stitch, increase the number of beads by 4 in Steps 1 and 2.

Chain Stitch Long-Short

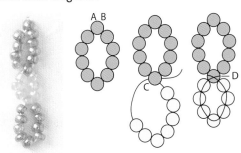

A B

C

D

1. Follow Step 1 of the chain stitch (at left) using 9 beads.

2. *Come up at **C** and stitch through the middle bead of the previous loop. Thread 7 (short) or 9 (long) size 11° seed beads onto the needle and lay the beads flat against the fabric.

3. Stitch through the middle bead again and down through the fabric at **D**. Knot the thread.

4. To finish the row, continue from * through the middle bead of the previous loop, alternating the number of beads from 9 (long) to 7 (short).

Chain Stitch Continuous Loops

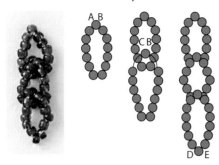  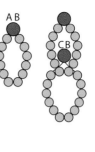 

1. Come up at **A**. *Thread 13 size 11° seed beads onto the needle and lay the beads flat against the fabric. Take the needle back through the first bead. Go down at **B**. Knot the thread.

2. To finish the row, stitch the needle up at **C** and repeat from *.

3. To end the stitch, follow Step 1 from * but with 14 size 11° seed beads. Come up at **D**; stitch through the middle bead and down through the fabric at **E**. Knot the thread.

Note: *To make a longer stitch, increase the number of beads by 4.*

Chain Stitch Continuous Loops Fancy

1. Come up at **A**. *Thread 1 size 8° and 12 size 11° seed beads onto the needle. Lay the beads flat against the fabric. Take the needle back through the size 8° bead. Go down at **B**. Knot the thread.

2. To finish the row, stitch the needle up through the loop at **C** and repeat from *.

3. To end the stitch, follow Step 1 with 1 size 8° and 13 size 11° seed beads. Come up at **D**; stitch through the middle bead and down through the fabric at **E**. Knot the thread.

Note: *To make a longer stitch, increase the number of size 11° beads by 4.*

Double Bubble Stitch

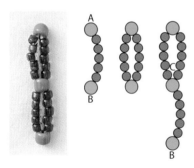

1. Come up at **A**. Thread 1 size 8°, 5 size 11°, and 1 size 8° seed beads onto the needle. *Lay the beads flat against the fabric. Go down at **B**.

2. Come back through the first size 8° bead in the row. Thread 5 size 11° seed beads and pass the needle through the next size 8° bead in the row. Go down through the fabric. Knot the thread.

3. To continue the row, come up at **C** and pass the needle through the last size 8° bead in the previous row. Thread 5 size 11° and 1 size 8° seed beads onto the needle. Follow Step 1 from *.

Cable Stitch

1. Work a row of chain stitches (page 47) using size 11° beads. Go back to the beginning of the row. *Come up through the loop at **C**, thread 5 size 11° seed beads onto the needle, and pass them down to the fabric. Go down at **D**. Knot the thread.

2. Repeat from * for each remaining loop.

Note: *The loop can also be made with 7 size 15° seed beads.*

FLY AND FEATHER STITCHES

Fly Stitch

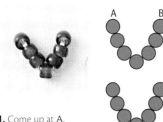 

1. Come up at **A**. Thread 7 size 11° seed beads onto the needle and lay the beads flat against the fabric. Go down at **B**. Knot the thread.

2. Come up at **C**, stitch through the middle bead, and go down at **D**. Knot the thread.

Note: *To make a longer stitch, increase the number of beads by 4. A different color or larger bead can be used for the middle bead in the loop.*

Fly Stitch with Loop

1. Follow Step 1 of the fly stitch (at left) but with 10 size 11° seed beads.

2. Come up at **C**. Thread 5 size 11° seed beads onto the needle and lay the beads flat against the fabric.

3. Go down at **D**. Knot the thread.

Note: *To make a longer stitch, increase the number of beads in Step 1 by 4. The loop in Step 2 can also be made with 7 size 15° seed beads.*

Fly Stitch with Tail

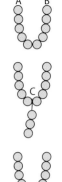 

1. Follow Step 1 of the fly stitch (at left) but with 10 size 11° seed beads.

2. Come up at **C**. Thread 3 size 11° seed beads onto the needle and lay the beads flat against the fabric.

3. Lay the thread between the fifth and sixth beads in the stitch. Go down at **D**. Knot the thread.

Note: *To make a longer stitch, increase the number of beads in Step 1 by 4 and in Step 2 by 2.*

Fly Stitch Fancy

 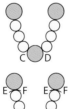

1. Come up at **A**. Thread 1 size 8°, 3 size 11°, 1 size 8°, 3 size 11°, and 1 size 8° seed beads onto the needle. Lay the beads flat against the fabric. Go down at **B**. Knot the thread.

2. Come up at **C**, stitch through the middle bead, and go down at **D**. Knot the thread.

3. Come up at **E**, between the size 8° and 11° beads, and go down at **F** to couch the bead thread. Knot the thread.

Note: *To make a longer stitch, increase the number of size 11° beads by 2 each time.*

Fly Stitch Fancy with Loop or Tail

 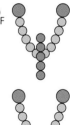

1. Come up at **A**. Thread 1 size 8°, 10 size 11°, and 1 size 8° seed beads onto the needle. Lay the beads flat against the fabric. Go down at **B**. Knot the thread. Follow Step 3 of the fly stitch fancy (at left).

2. Follow Steps 2 and 3 of the fly stitch with loop (above center) or fly stitch with tail (above right).

Fly Stitch with Larger Beads

 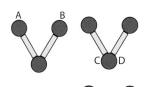

1. Come up at **A**. Thread 1 size 8° seed bead, 1 bugle bead, 1 size 8° seed bead, 1 bugle bead, and 1 size 8° seed bead onto the needle. Lay the beads flat against the fabric. Go down at **B**. Knot the thread.

2. Come up at **C**, stitch through the size 8° bead, and go down at **D**. Knot the thread.

3. Come up at **E**, between the size 8° bead and the bugle bead, and go down at **F** to couch the bead thread. Knot the thread.

Fly Stitch Border Rows

A. Up or down, **B.** Up-down mix, **C.** Wave

Follow the directions for the any of the fly stitches (page 49 and this page), working the stitches along a seam or drawn line.

Feather Stitch

1. Come up at **A**. *Thread 9 size 11° seed beads onto the needle and lay the beads flat against the fabric. Go down to the right at **B**. Knot the thread. Come up at **C** and stitch through the middle bead from right to left.

2. Follow Step 1 from *. Go down to the left at **B**. When you come up at **C**, stitch through the middle bead from left to right.

3. To finish the row, alternate stitches to the left and to the right. To end the stitch, come up at **C**, stitch through the middle bead, and go down at **D**. Knot the thread.

Note: *To make a longer stitch, increase the number of beads by 4.*

Feather Stitch Single

1. Come up at **A**. *Thread 10 size 11° seed beads onto the needle and lay the beads flat against the fabric. Go down to the right at **B**, slightly below **A**. Knot the thread.

2. To finish the row, come up at **C**. Follow Step 1 from *, laying the thread between the fifth and sixth beads of the previous stitch.

3. To end the stitch, follow Step 1 from * but with 11 size 11° seed beads. Come up at **D**; stitch through the middle bead and down through the fabric at **E**. Knot the thread.

Note: *This stitch can be worked with the tips facing right or left.*

Feather Stitch with Loops

1. Come up at **A**. *Thread 12 size 11° seed beads onto the needle and lay the beads flat against the fabric. Go down to the right at **B**. Knot the thread.

2. Come up at **C**. Follow Step 1 from *, with the needle in the center of the stitch, close to the previous loop of beads. Go down to the left at **B**.

3. Come up at **C**. To finish the row, alternate between Steps 1 and 2.

4. To end the stitch, follow from * with 13 size 11° seed beads. Come up at **D**, stitch through the middle bead, and go down at **E**. Knot the thread.

Note: *To make a longer stitch, increase the number of beads in Step 1 by 4.*

Feather Stitch Fancy

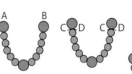

1. Come up at **A**. *Thread 1 size 8°, 5 size 11°, 1 size 8°, 5 size 11°, and 1 size 8° seed beads onto the needle. Lay the beads flat against the fabric. Go down to the right at **B**. Knot the thread.

2. Come up at **C**, between the size 8° and 11° beads, and go down at **D** to couch the bead thread. Knot the thread.

3. Come up at **E**. Stitch through the size 8° bead from right to left. Thread 5 size 11°, 1 size 8°, 5 size 11°, and 1 size 8° seed beads onto the needle. Lay the beads flat against the fabric. Go down to the left at **B**. Knot the thread. Follow Step 2.

4. To finish the row, alternate stitches to the right and to the left. To end the stitch, come up at **E**, stitch through the middle bead, and go down at **F**. Knot the thread.

Note: *To make a longer stitch, increase the number of all size 11° beads by 2 each time.*

Kelp Stitch

1. Follow Step 1 of the feather stitch fancy (above right).

2. Come up at **E** and *stitch through the middle size 8° seed bead from left to right. Thread 5 size 11° and 1 size 8° seed beads onto the needle. Lay the beads flat against the fabric. Go down at **B**. Knot the thread. Follow Step 2 for the feather stitch fancy.

3. Come up at **F**, and follow Step 3 of the feather stitch fancy. Come up at **F** and repeat from * (above), right to left.

4. To finish the row, alternate stitches to the right and to the left. To end the stitch, come up at **F**, stitch through the middle size 8° seed bead, and go down at **G**. Knot the thread.

Feather Stitch with Larger Beads

1. Come up at **A**. *Thread 1 size 11° seed bead, 1 bugle bead, 3 size 11° seed beads, 1 bugle bead, and 1 size 11° seed bead onto the needle. Lay the beads flat against the fabric. Go down to the right at **B**. Knot the thread.

2. Come up at **C**, between the size 11° bead and the bugle bead, and go down at **D** to couch the bead thread. Knot the thread.

3. Come up at **E** and stitch through the middle size 11° bead to the left. Follow Step 1 from *, and go down to the left.

4. To finish the row, alternate stitches to the right and to the left. To end the stitch, come up at **E**, stitch through the middle bead, and go down at **F**. Knot the thread.

CONTINUOUS BEAD AND BLANKET STITCHES

Continuous Bead Stitch Straight

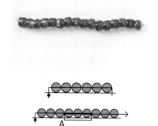

1. Come up and *thread 6 beads onto the needle; lay the beads flat against the fabric. Go down just beyond the edge of the last bead.

2. Come up at **A**, between the third and fourth bead in the row. Thread the needle through the remaining 3 beads in the row. To finish the row, continue from *.

3. To end the stitch, come up at **A**, go through the last 3 beads in the row, and go down at **B**. Knot the thread.

Note: *If the line of beads is not straight, pass the needle through the entire row of beads a second time.*

Continuous Bead Stitch Curved

Draw a curved line with an air-erasable marking pen. Follow the directions for the continuous bead stitch straight (at left), using 4 beads instead of 6.

Note: *If the beads do not lie flat, start at the beginning and couch every 4 beads to the end of the row.*

Continuous Bead Stitch Fancy

1. Come up and *thread 3 size 11° and 1 size 8° seed beads onto the needle. Lay the beads flat against the fabric. Go down just beyond the edge of the last bead.

2. Come up at **A**, between the second and third size 11° seed beads in the row. Thread the needle through the size 11° and the size 8° seed beads. To finish the row, continue from *.

3. To end the row, come up at **A**, go through the last 2 beads in the row, and go down at **B**. Knot the thread.

Spine Vine Stitch

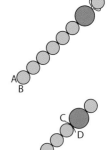

1. Come up at **A** and *thread 6 size 11°, 1 size 8°, and 1 size 11° seed beads onto the needle. Lay the beads flat against the fabric. Pass the needle through the size 8° bead and the remaining beads in the row. Go down at **B**. Knot the thread.

2. Come up at **C**, between the size 8° and 11° beads, and go down at **D** to couch the bead thread. Knot the thread.

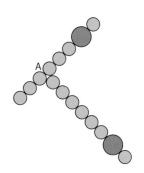

3. Come up at **A** and pass the needle through the first 3 beads in the previous row. To finish the row, repeat from *.

Continuous Bead Stitch Picot Tip

1. Work a row of continuous bead stitches (previous page) using size 11° seed beads. Come up at **A** and go through the first 2 beads at the beginning of the row. *Thread 3 size 11° seed beads onto the needle. Skip 1 bead and thread the needle through the next 2 beads in the row.

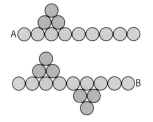

2. To finish the row, continue from *. To end the stitch, go through the remaining beads in the row. Go down at **B**. Knot the thread.

Continuous Bead Stitch Knobbed

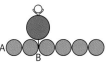

1. Work a row of continuous bead stitches (previous page) using size 11° seed beads.

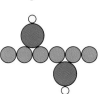

2. Come up at **A** and go through the first 2 beads at the beginning of the row. *Thread 1 size 8° and 1 size 15° seed bead onto the needle. Thread the needle back through the size 8° seed bead and down through the fabric at **B**. Knot the thread.

3. Come up close to **B**. Thread the needle through the next 2 beads in the row. To finish the row, continue from *, working the stitches on either side of the row.

Beaded Vine Stitch

1. Work a row of continuous bead stitches (previous page) using size 11° seed beads.

2. Come up at **A** and go through the first 3 beads at the beginning of the row. *Thread 1 size 8° and 9 size 11° seed beads onto the needle. Thread the needle back through the size 8° seed bead and down through the fabric at **B**. Knot the thread.

3. Come up close to **B**. Thread the needle through the next 3 beads in the row. To finish the row, continue from *.

Blanket Stitch Even

1. Work a row of continuous bead stitches (previous page).

2. Come up at **A** and go through the first 3 beads at the beginning of the row. **Spoke:** *Thread 3 size 11° seed beads onto the needle and lay the beads flat against the fabric. Go down at **B**. Knot the thread.

3. Come up at **C**. Thread the needle back through the spoke and through the next 3 beads in the row. To finish the row, continue from *.

Blanket Stitch Short-Long

Follow the directions for the blanket stitch even (above right) but alternate the spokes between 3 and 5 beads.

Blanket Stitch Up-Down

Follow the directions for the blanket stitch even (above) but work 2 spokes, alternating on either side of the continuous stitch base.

Blanket Stitch Frilled

Follow the directions for the blanket stitch even (page 53) using these suggestions. Use size 11° seed beads unless otherwise noted. Follow the couching directions in Step 2 of the bead combination stitch (page 64).

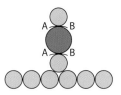

1 size 11°, 1 size 8°, and 1 size 11° seed beads.

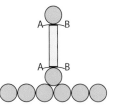

1 size 11° seed bead, 1 bugle bead, and 1 size 11° seed bead.

Blanket Stitch Angled

Follow the directions for the blanket stitch even (page 53), angling the spokes and alternating them on either side of the continuous stitch straight or curved base.

Blanket Stitch Fancy

1. Work a row of continuous bead stitch fancy (page 52). *Come up at **A** and go through the size 8° bead in the previous row. **Spoke:** Thread 3 size 11° and 1 size 8° seed beads onto the needle. Lay the beads flat against the fabric. Go down at **B**. Knot the thread.

2. Come up at **C**, between the size 11° and size 8° beads, and go down at **D** to couch the bead thread.

3. To finish the row, continue from *.

Beaded Vine Stitch Fancy

1. Work a row of continuous bead stitch fancy (page 52). *Come up at **A** and go through the size 8° seed bead in the previous row. Thread 4 size 11°, 1 size 8°, and 4 size 11° seed beads onto the needle. Lay the beads flat against the fabric. Thread the needle back through the size 8° seed bead. Go down at **B**. Knot the thread.

2. Come up at **C**, stitch through the size 8° seed bead, and go down at **D**. Knot the thread.

3. To finish the row, continue from *.

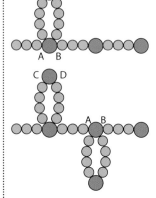

CROSS, HERRINGBONE, SERPENTINE, AND CRETAN STITCHES

Cross Stitch

 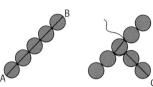

1. Come up at **A**. Thread 5 size 11° seed beads onto the needle and lay the beads flat against the fabric. Go down at **B**. Knot the thread.

2. Come up at **C**. Thread 2 size 11° seed beads onto the needle and lay the beads flat against the fabric. Pass the needle from bottom to top through the middle bead in the previous row.

Note: This changes the direction of the bead.

3. Thread 2 size 11° seed beads onto the needle, lay the beads flat against the fabric, and go down at **D**. Knot the thread.

Jacks Stitch

 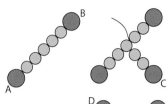

1. Come up at **A**. Thread 1 size 8°, 5 size 11°, and 1 size 8° seed beads onto the needle. Lay the beads flat against the fabric. Go down at **B**. Knot the thread.

2. Come up at **C**. Thread 1 size 8° and 2 size 11° seed beads onto the needle. Lay the beads flat against the fabric. Pass the needle from bottom to top through the middle bead in the previous row. (See the note in Cross Stitch, at left.)

3. Thread 2 size 11° and 1 size 8° seed beads onto the needle. Lay the beads flat against the fabric. Go down at **D**. Knot the thread.

Cross Stitch with Center

 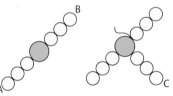

1. Come up at **A**. Thread 3 size 11°, 1 size 8°, and 3 size 11° seed beads onto the needle. Lay the beads flat against the fabric. Go down at **B**. Knot the thread.

2. Come up at **C**. Thread 3 size 11° seed beads onto the needle and lay the beads flat against the fabric. Pass the needle from bottom to top through the middle bead in the previous row. (See the note in Cross Stitch, above.)

3. Thread 3 size 11° seed beads onto the needle and lay the beads flat against the fabric. Go down at **D**. Knot the thread.

Note: This stitch can also be worked with 2 colors of size 11° seed beads.

Cross Stitch Row

1. Follow Step 1 of the cross stitch (above left). Repeat this stitch to the end of the row.

2. Follow Steps 2 and 3 of the cross stitch. Repeat this stitch to the end of the row.

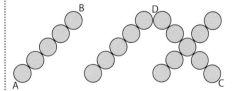

Cross Stitch Long Arm Row

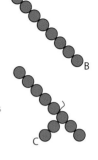

1. Come up at **A**. Thread 1 size 8°, 3 size 11°, 1 size 8°, 3 size 11°, and 1 size 8° seed beads onto the needle. Lay the beads flat against the fabric. Go down at **B**. Knot the thread.

2. *Come up at **C**. Thread 1 size 8° and **3 size 11° seed beads onto the needle. Lay the beads flat against the fabric. Pass the needle from bottom to top through the size 8° bead in the previous row. (See the note in Cross Stitch, page 55.)

3. Thread 3 size 11° and 1 size 8° seed beads onto the needle. Lay the beads flat against the fabric. Go down at **D**. Knot the thread.

4. Come up at **E** and pass the needle through the size 8° bead in the previous row. (See the note in Cross Stitch, page 55.) Thread 3 size 11°, 1 size 8°, 3 size 11°, and 1 size 8° seed beads onto the needle. Lay the beads flat against the fabric. Go down at **B**. Knot the thread.

5. To finish the row, come up at **F** and pass through the size 8° bead in the previous row; repeat from **.

Herringbone Stitch

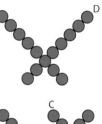

1. Come up at **A**. Thread 8 size 11° seed beads onto the needle and lay the beads flat against the fabric. Go down at **B**. Knot the thread.

2. *Come up at **C**. Thread 2 size 11° seed beads onto the needle and lay the beads flat against the fabric. Pass the needle from either top or bottom through the third bead in the previous row. (See the note in Cross Stitch, page 55.)

3. Thread 5 size 11° seed beads onto the needle and lay the beads flat against the fabric. Go down at **D**. Knot the thread.

4. To finish the row, repeat from *.

Herringbone Stitch with Center

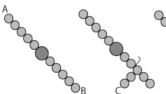

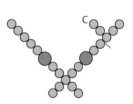

1. Come up at **A**. Thread 5 size 11°, 1 size 8°, and 5 size 11° seed beads onto the needle. Lay the beads flat against the fabric. Go down at **B**. Knot the thread.

2. *Come up at **C**. Thread 2 size 11° seed beads onto the needle and lay the beads flat against the fabric. Pass the needle from either top or bottom through the third bead in the previous row. (See the note in Cross Stitch, page 55.)

3. Thread 2 size 11°, 1 size 8°, and 5 size 11° seed beads onto the needle. Lay the beads flat against the fabric. Go down at **D**. Knot the thread.

4. To finish the row, repeat from *.

Serpentine Stitch Curved

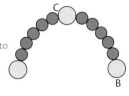

1. Come up at **A**. Thread 1 size 8°, 5 size 11°, and 1 size 8° seed beads onto the needle. Lay the beads flat against the fabric. Go down at **B**. Knot the thread.

2. *Come up at **C**. Pass the needle through the size 8° bead in the previous row. Thread 5 size 11° and 1 size 8° seed beads onto the needle. Lay the beads flat against the fabric. Go down at **B**. Knot the thread.

3. To finish the row, repeat from *.

Serpentine Stitch V Shape

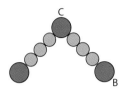

1. Come up at **A**. Thread 1 size 8°, 3 size 11°, and 1 size 8° seed beads onto the needle. Lay the beads flat against the fabric. Go down at **B**. Knot the thread.

2. *Come up at **C**. (See the note in Cross Stitch, page 55.) Pass the needle through the size 8° bead in the previous row. Thread 3 size 11° and 1 size 8° seed beads onto the needle. Lay the beads flat against the fabric. Go down at **B**. Knot the thread.

3. To finish the row, repeat from *.

Serpentine Stitch Fancy

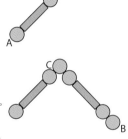

1. Come up at **A**. *Thread 1 size 11° seed bead, 1 bugle bead, and 2 size 11° seed beads onto the needle. Lay the beads flat against the fabric. Go down at **B**. Knot the thread.

2. Come up at **C**. Pass the needle through the second size 11° bead in the previous row. (See the note in Cross Stitch, page 55.)

3. To finish the row, repeat from *.

Serpentine Stitch with Sequins

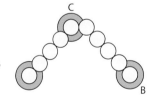

1. Come up at **A**. Thread 1 sequin, 5 size 11° seed beads, and 1 sequin onto the needle. Lay the sequins and beads flat against the fabric. Go down at **B**. Knot the thread.

2. *Come up at **C**. Pass the needle through the sequin in the previous row. Thread 5 size 11° seed beads and 1 sequin onto the needle. Lay the sequins and beads flat against the fabric. Go down at **B**. Knot the thread.

3. To finish the row, repeat from *.

Note: *A, B, and C are underneath the sequin.*

Cretan Stitch Looped

1. Follow Step 1 of the serpentine stitch V shape (page 57) with 5 size 11° seed beads.

2. *Come up at **C**. (See the note in Cross Stitch, page 55.) Pass the needle through the size 8° bead in the previous row. Thread 5 size 15° seed beads onto the needle and lay the beads flat against the fabric. Pass the needle back through the size 8° bead.

3. Thread 5 size 11° and 1 size 8° seed beads onto the needle. Lay the beads flat against the fabric. Go down at **B**. Knot the thread.

4. To finish the row, repeat from *.

Cretan Stitch with Tip

1. Come up at **A**. Thread 2 size 11°, 1 size 8°, 3 size 11°, 1 size 8°, and 2 size 11° seed beads onto the needle. Lay the beads flat against the fabric. Go down at **B**. Knot the thread.

2. *Come up at **C**. Pass the needle through the size 8° bead in the previous row. (See the note in Cross Stitch, page 55.) Thread 3 size 11°, 1 size 8°, and 2 size 11° seed beads onto the needle. Lay the beads flat against the fabric. Go down at **B**. Knot the thread.

3. To finish the row, repeat from *.

Cretan Stitch Fancy

   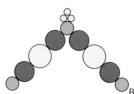

1. Come up at **A**. Thread 1 size 11°, 1 size 8°, 1 size 6°, 1 size 8°, and 1 size 11° seed beads onto the needle. Lay the beads flat against the fabric. Go down at **B**. Knot the thread.

2. *Come up at **C**. Pass the needle through the size 11° bead in the previous row. (See the note in Cross Stitch, page 55.) Thread 3 size 15° seed beads onto the needle and lay the beads flat against the fabric. Pass the needle back through the size 11° bead.

3. Thread 1 size 8°, 1 size 6°, 1 size 8°, and 1 size 11° seed beads onto the needle. Lay the beads flat against the fabric. Go down at **B**. Knot the thread.

4. To finish the row, repeat from *.

FLOWERS AND EXTRA STITCHES

Flowers with Petals

You can use any number of centers, petals, and stitch combinations to create a flower.

1. Use the templates and an air-erasable marking pen to draw the flower shape.

2. Stitch the center of the flower first; then stitch in each petal following the directions for the stitch listed.

FLOWER WITH STRAIGHT PETALS

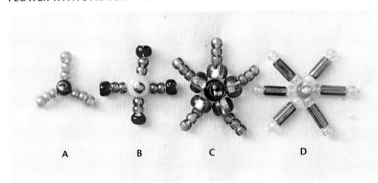

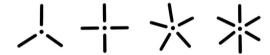

These stitches were used in the following examples: stacked bead stitch (page 64), grouped bead stitch (page 64), bead combination stitch (page 64), and picot tip stitch (page 65).

A. Center: Stacked bead stitch, size 8° and 15° seed beads. **Petals:** Grouped bead stitch, size 11° seed beads.

B. Center: Stacked bead stitch, size 6° and 11° seed beads. **Petals:** Bead combination stitch, size 8° and 11° seed beads.

C. Center: Picot tip stitch, size 6° and 15° seed beads. **Petals:** Bead combination stitch, size 6° and 11° seed beads.

D. Center: Stacked bead stitch, size 8° and 11° seed beads. **Petals:** Bead combination stitch, size 11° seed beads and bugle beads.

FLOWER WITH PETITE PETALS

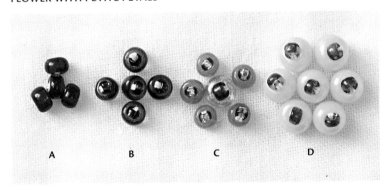

These stitches were used in the following examples: single bead stitch (page 64) and stacked bead stitch (page 64).

A. Center and petals: Single bead stitch, size 8° seed beads.

B. Center and petals: Stacked bead stitch, size 8° and 15° seed beads.

C. Center: Stacked bead stitch, size 6° and 11° seed beads. **Petals:** Stacked bead stitch, size 8° and 15° seed beads.

D. Center and petals: Stacked bead stitch, size 6° and 11° seed beads.

FLOWER WITH LAZY DAISY PETALS

These stitches were used in the following examples: beaded stamen stitch (page 66), lazy daisy stitch (page 46), picot tip stitch (page 65), lazy daisy stitch fancy (page 46), stacked bead stitch (page 64), lazy daisy stitch with loop (page 46), beaded pistil stitch (page 66), and lazy daisy stitch loose (page 46).

A. Center: Beaded stamen stitch, size 11° seed beads.
Petals: Lazy daisy stitch, size 11° seed beads.

B. Center: Picot tip stitch, size 8° and 15° seed beads.
Petals: Lazy daisy stitch fancy, size 8° and 11° seed beads.

C. Center: Stacked bead stitch, size 6° and 11° seed beads.
Petals: Lazy daisy stitch with loop, size 11° seed beads.

D. Center: Beaded pistil stitch, size 11° seed beads and 4mm round bead. **Petals:** Lazy daisy stitch loose, size 11° seed beads.

FLOWER WITH FLY STITCH PETALS

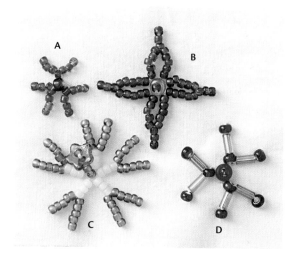

These stitches were used in the following examples: single bead stitch (page 64), fly stitch (page 49), stacked bead stitch (page 64), fly stitch with tail (page 49), stem and flower stitch (page 66), and fly stitch with larger beads (page 50).

A. Center: Single bead stitch, size 8° seed bead.
Petals: Fly stitch, size 11° seed beads.

B. Center: Stacked bead stitch, size 6° and 11° seed beads.
Petals: Fly stitch with tail, size 11° seed beads.

C. Center: Stem and flower stitch, size 11° seed beads and flower rondelle. **Petals:** Fly stitch with tail, size 11° seed beads.

D. Center: Stacked bead stitch, size 6° and 11° seed beads. **Petals:** Fly stitch with larger beads, size 8° seed beads and bugle beads.

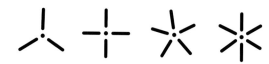

French Rose Stitch

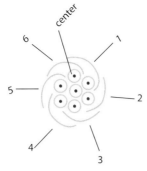

1. Work 7 stacked bead stitches (page 64) with size 8° and 15° seed beads. Knot the thread. Come up at **A**. *Thread 8 size 11° seed beads onto the needle and go down at **B**. Knot the thread.

2. Repeat from * for the remaining petals, with **A** beginning behind the previous petal. *Note:* For the last petal, **B** ends inside the first petal.

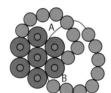

Small French Rose Stitch

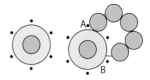

1. Work a stacked bead stitch (page 64) with 1 size 6° and 1 size 11° seed beads. Knot the thread. With an air-erasable pen, draw the 6 points shown, slightly away from the center bead.

2. Come up at **A** at the first point. *Thread 5 size 11° seed beads onto the needle and go down at **B** next to the center bead. Knot the thread.

3. Repeat from * for the remaining petals, with **A** beginning behind the previous petal. *Note:* For the last petal, **B** ends inside the first petal. Knot the thread.

Floret Stitch

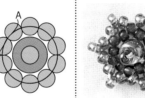

1. Center: Work a stacked bead stitch (page 64) with 1 size 6° and 1 size 11° seed bead. Come up at **A**.

2. Bezel: Thread enough size 11° seed beads (10–12) to wrap around the size 6° bead. Pass the needle through the first 2 beads in the row and through the remaining beads in the bezel. Go down at **B**. Knot the thread.

3. Come up at **C**, between 2 beads, and go down at **D** to couch the bead thread. Repeat this step every 2 beads in the row. Knot the thread.

Floret Star Stitch

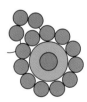

1. Work a floret stitch (at left) with a bezel of 12 size 11° seed beads. Knot the thread. Come up through the fabric and a bead in the bezel.

2. Points: *Thread 3 size 11° seed beads onto the needle. Skip 1 bead in the bezel, and pass the needle through the next bead. Continue from *. Go down after the last point. Knot the thread.

Daisy Stitch

1. Center: Follow Step 1 of the floret stitch (page 61).

2. Bezel: Follow Step 2 of the floret stitch (page 61), with 8–10 size 8° seed beads.

3. Petals: Come up through a bead in the bezel. *Thread 7 size 11° seed beads onto the needle. Pass the needle back through the same bead and down through the fabric. Knot the thread.

4. To finish the flower, continue from *.

Hippie Flower Stitch

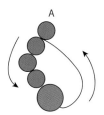

1. Come up at **A**. Thread 4 size 11° and 1 size 8° seed beads onto the needle. *Pass the needle from left to right through the first size 11° bead in the row. (See note in Cross Stitch, page 55.) Go down at **A**.

2. Come up at **B**. Follow from *, and thread 3 size 11° seed beads onto the needle. Pass the needle from right to left through the last size 11° bead in the beginning row. Go down at **C**. Knot the thread.

Knot Stitch

1. Come up at **A**. Thread 3 size 8° seed beads onto the needle. Pass the needle through the first bead in the row. Go down at **B**.

2. Come up at **C**, pass the needle through the bead, and go down at **D**. Repeat this step for the next bead in the row.

3. Come up at **E** and pass the needle through a bead. *Thread 3 size 11° seed beads onto the needle and pass the needle through the next bead in the row. Repeat from * for each remaining bead. Go down at **F**. Knot the thread.

Tiny Flower Stitch

1. Come up at **A**. Thread 5 size 11° seed beads onto the needle. Pass the needle through the first bead and the remaining beads in the row. Go down at **B**.

2. Come up at **C** and go down at **D** to couch the bead thread. Repeat for each bead. Knot the thread.

Spindle Star Stitch

1. Center: Work a tiny flower stitch (previous page) with size 11° seed beads.

2. Spindle: *Come up at **A**. Thread 4 size 11° seed beads onto the needle, pass the needle through 1 bead in the center, and go back through the beads of the spindle. Go down at **B**. Knot the thread.

3. Repeat from * for each remaining spindle.

Snail Stitch

1. Cut a small square of Décor-Bond. Use the diagram and an air-erasable marking pen to draw the snail shell. Use the shape as a guide.

2. Stitch a single bead stitch (page 64) with a size 8° seed bead. Knot the thread.
*Come up next to the size 8° bead and thread 4 size 11° seed beads onto the needle.

3. Follow the directions for the continuous bead stitch curved (page 52). Continue to work the stitch with 25 or more beads, wrapping the curve tightly around the size 8° bead.

4. Trim off the excess Décor-Bond.

Spider Web Stitch

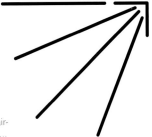

1. Use the diagram and an air-erasable marking pen to draw the web shape.

2. Work the stitches in the following order:

   A. At the center of the web, work a stacked bead stitch (page 64), using size 6° and 11° seed beads.

   B. Work each spoke with the continuous bead stitch (page 52), using size 11° seed beads.

   C. Work each connector spoke with the continuous bead stitch, using size 11° seed beads.

Anemone Stitch

1. Center: Work a stacked bead stitch (page 64) with 1 size 6° and 1 size 11° seed beads. Use an air-erasable marking pen to draw in 6 points.

2. Petals: Work a beaded pistil stitch (page 66), using 4 size 11° seed beads for each point.

DECORATIVE AND DETAIL STITCHES

Single Bead Stitch

 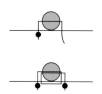

1. Come up and thread 1 bead onto the needle. Lay the bead flat against the fabric. Go down beyond the edge of the bead.

2. Come up and pass the needle through the bead a second time and down. Knot the thread after every 4 stitches.

Grouped Bead Stitch

Follow the directions for the single bead stitch (at left) but with 2 or 3 of the same size and type of bead. Knot the thread after every 2 stitches.

Bead Combination Stitch

 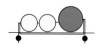

1. Follow the directions for the single bead stitch (above) but with a group of different sizes or shapes of beads.

2. Come up at **A**, between the large and small beads, and go down at **B** to couch the bead thread. Knot the thread after every 2 stitches.

Stacked Bead Stitch

1. Base bead: Come through a large bead.

2. Stopper bead: Thread a smaller bead onto the needle. Holding onto the bead, pass the needle back down through the base bead and down. Knot the thread.

Picot Tip Stitch

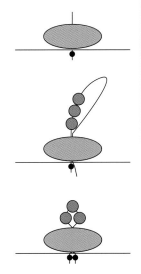

1. Base bead: Come up through a large bead.

2. Picot tip: Thread 3 smaller beads onto the needle. Holding onto the 3 beads, pass the needle back down through the base bead and down. Knot the thread.

Bead Cascade Stitch

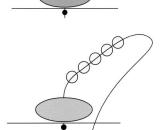

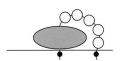

1. Base bead: Come up through a large bead.

2. Cascade: Thread 3–7 or more smaller beads onto the needle and go down just beyond the edge of the larger bead. Knot the thread.

Bird Tracks Border Row Stitch

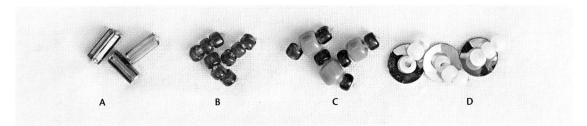

A. Single bead stitch, **B.** Grouped bead stitch, **C.** Bead combination stitch, **D.** Bead cascade stitch

Follow the directions for the single bead (previous page), grouped bead (previous page), bead combination (previous page), or bead cascade (above right) stitch, working the stitches along a seam or drawn line and alternating the stitches on either side of the line or seam. Knot the thread after every 2 stitches.

Beaded Stamen Stitch

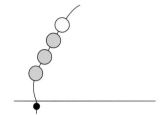

1. Come up and thread 4 or more size 11° seed beads onto the needle.

2. Holding onto the last bead(s), pass the needle through the remaining beads and down. Knot the thread.

Note: *The last bead can be 1–3 of the same bead or smaller.*

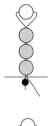

Beaded Pistil Stitch

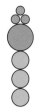

1. Come up and thread 3–5 size 11° seed beads, 1 size 8° seed bead or a 4 mm round bead, and 1–3 size 15° seed beads onto the needle.

2. Holding onto the last bead(s), pass the needle through the remaining beads and down. Knot the thread.

Stem and Flower Stitch

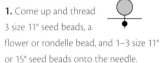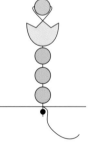

1. Come up and thread 3 size 11° seed beads, a flower or rondelle bead, and 1–3 size 11° or 15° seed beads onto the needle.

2. Holding onto the last bead(s), pass the needle through the remaining beads and down. Knot the thread.

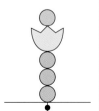

Front-to-Back Hole Charm Stitch

Come up through the hole in the charm and follow the directions for the stopper bead in Step 2 of stacked bead stitch (page 64).

Or come up through the hole of the charm and follow the directions for the cascade in Step 2 of bead cascade stitch (page 65).

Top-to-Bottom Hole Charm Stitch

Follow the directions for the bead combination stitch (page 64), with the charm in the middle of the group; couch on either side of the charm. Knot the thread.

Side-to-Side Hole Charm Stitch

Follow the directions for the bead combination stitch (page 64), with the charm in the middle of the group; couch on either side of the charm. Knot the thread.

Front-to-Back Hole Charm Dangle Stitch

1. Thread 1 size 8° seed bead, 1 size 6° seed bead, 3–9 size 11° seed beads, 1 charm, and the same amount of size 11° seed beads onto the needle.

2. Holding onto the charm, pass the needle back through the size 6° and remaining beads and go down. Knot the thread.

Note: *The bead design can be longer if desired.*

Top-to-Bottom Hole Charm Dangle Stitch

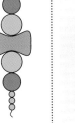

1. Thread 1 size 8° seed bead, 1 size 6° seed bead, 1 charm or rondelle, 1 size 6° seed bead, 1 size 8° seed bead, and 3 size 11° or size 15° seed beads onto the needle.

2. Holding onto the last 3 seed beads, pass the needle back through the remaining beads in the row and go down. Knot the thread.

Note: *The bead design can be longer if desired.*

Side-to-Side Hole Charm Dangle Stitch

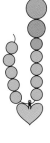
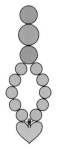

1. Thread 1 size 8° seed bead, 1 size 6° seed bead, 1 size 8° seed bead, 5–9 size 11° seed beads, 1 charm, and 5–9 size 11° seed beads onto the needle.

2. Holding onto the charm, pass the needle back through the size 8° seed bead and the remaining beads in the row and go down. Knot the thread.

Note: *The bead design can be longer if desired.*

BUTTON AND SEQUIN FLOWERS

Button Hole Decoration Stitches

You can use any number of centers to decorate the center of a button.

Stitch through the button with beading thread or perle cotton #8 to hold it in place. Follow the directions for the stitch listed.

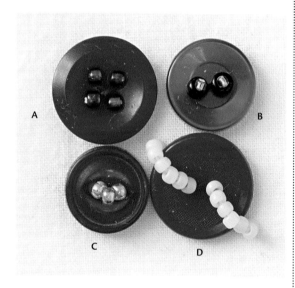

A. Button holes with single beads (page 64) using size 11°, 8°, or 6° seed beads.

B. Button holes with stacked beads (page 64) using size 8° and 15° seed beads or size 6° and 11° seed beads.

C. Button holes stitched with a grouped bead stitch (page 64) using 3 or 4 size 11° seed beads.

D. Button holes with a bead cascade stitch (page 65) using size 11° seed beads.

Note: *To keep a button with a wire shank from moving, thread a size 11° or 8° seed bead onto the needle before and after stitching through the shank.*

Button Bezel Stitch

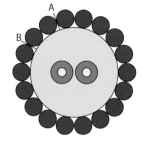

1. Stitch the center of the button in place, using any of the button hole decoration stitches (at left). Come up at **A**. Thread 4 size 11° seed beads onto the needle. Follow the directions for the continuous bead stitch curved (page 52).

2. Add the last group of beads; then pass the needle through the first 2 beads and the remaining beads in the row. Go down at **B**. Knot the thread.

Button Bezel Stitch with Picot Tip

1. Center: Work 2 stacked bead stitches (page 64) using size 8° and 15° seed beads.

2. Bezel: Follow the directions for the button bezel stitch (above) using an even amount of size 11° seed beads. Come up through the fabric and a bead in the bezel.

3. Picot tip: *Thread 3 size 11° seed beads onto the needle. Skipping 1 bead in the bezel, pass the needle through the next bead. Continue from *. Go down after the last picot tip. Knot the thread.

Button Sunflower Stitch

1. Center: Stitch a shank button to the fabric.

2. Bezel: Come up through the fabric close to the shank. Follow the directions for the bezel in the floret stitch (Step 2, page 61) using size 8° seed beads.

3. Come up through the fabric and a bead in the bezel.

4. Follow Steps 1 and 2 of the lazy daisy stitch with tip (page 46). Pass the needle back through the same bead in the bezel and down. Come up and pass the needle through the next bead in the bezel.

5. Repeat Step 4 (above) for each bead in the bezel. Go down after the last petal. Knot the thread.

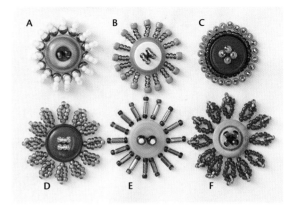

Button Flower with Petals Stitch

You can use any number of centers and petals to create a button flower.

1. Stitch the center of the button flower first.

2. Use an air-erasable marking pen to draw in 4 points as shown.

3. Draw in the remaining points, using **A** for full petals or **B** for straight petals.

4. Stitch in each petal following the directions for the stitch listed.

These stitches were used in the following examples: single bead stitch (page 64), bead cascade stitch (page 65), picot tip stitch (page 65), bead combination stitch (page 64), stacked bead stitch (page 64), button bezel stitch (previous page), lazy daisy stitch (page 46), and lazy daisy stitch with loop (page 46).

A. Button holes: Single bead stitch, size 8° seed beads.
Petals: Bead cascade stitch, size 6° and 11° seed beads.

B. Button holes: Picot tip stitch, size 11° seed beads.
Petals: Bead combination stitch, size 11° and 8° seed beads.

C. Button holes: Stacked bead stitch, size 8° and 15° seed beads.
Petals: Button bezel stitch, size 11° seed beads; stacked bead stitch, size 8° and 15° seed beads.

D. Button holes: Picot tip stitch, size 11° seed beads.
Petals: Lazy daisy stitch, size 11° seed beads.

E. Button holes: Stacked bead stitch, size 6° and 11° seed beads.
Petals: Bead combination stitch, size 11° seed and bugle beads.

F. Button holes: Single bead stitch, size 8° seed beads.
Petals: Lazy daisy stitch with loop, size 11° and 15° seed beads.

Spider Stitch

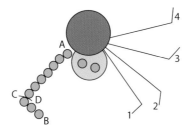

Legs 1 and 2: 10 size 15° seed beads,
Legs 3 and 4: 12 size 15° seed beads

1. Body: Stitch a ⅜" shank button for the body, using perle cotton or beading thread. Stitch a 2-hole ¼" button for the head.

2. Stitch 1 size 11° seed bead for each eye.

3. Legs: Come up at **A**, thread the number of size 15° seed beads as suggested, and go down at **B**. Come up at **C**, between the third and fourth bead at the end of the row, and go down at **D** to form a joint. Knot the thread. Repeat for each leg.

Note: *The button sizes can vary, or large beads can be substituted for the buttons. For longer spider legs, use more beads; for larger buttons, use size 11° seed beads for the legs.*

Sequin Decoration Stitches

You can stitch a sequin with any number of centers.

These stitches were used in the following examples: stacked bead stitch (page 64) and bead cascade stitch (page 65).

A. Stacked bead stitch with sequin and size 11° seed beads.

B. Stacked bead stitch with 2 different size sequins and size 11° seed beads.

C. Stacked bead stitch with sequin and size 6° and 11° seed beads.

D. Stacked bead stitch with 2 different size sequins and size 8° and 15° seed beads.

E. Bead cascade stitch with sequin and size 11° seed beads.

F. Bead cascade stitch with 2 different size sequins and size 11° seed beads.

Sequin Flowers

You can create a sequin flower from any number of centers and petals.

These stitches were used in the following examples: bead cascade stitch (page 65) and stacked bead stitch (page 64).

A. Center and petals: Bead cascade stitch with sequin and size 15° seed beads.

B. Center and petals: Bead cascade stitch with sequin, size 15° seed beads, and sequin.

C. Center and petals: Stacked bead stitch with sequin and size 15° seed beads.

D. Center and petals: Stacked bead stitch with sequin and size 8° and 15° seed beads.

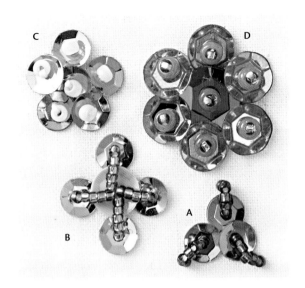

Sequin Rose Stitch

1. Draw a ½″ circle with an air-erasable pen. Come up on the line. *Follow the directions for the stacked bead stitch (page 64), using a sequin and a size 11° or 15° seed bead. Continue around the line, repeating from *.

2. Come inside the first row of sequins. Repeat from *, stitching 3–4 sequins in the center of the ring.

Sequin Rose Stitch Variation

Follow the directions for the sequin rose stitch (at left), using the bead cascade stitch (page 65) with a sequin and 3–5 size 11° or 15° seed beads.

BEADED EDGES

Thread and Needle Specifics

The following beaded edge designs can be used to decorate the edge of a piece of fabric or ribbon. For a ribbon rosette or a fabric yo-yo, use thread option 1. For the edge of a fabric brooch or a wallhanging or to sew together the two edges of a ribbon bracelet, use thread option 2.

Thread option 1: Cut 1 yard of beading thread. Thread the needle, using the thread single. Wax and knot the tail.

Thread option 2: Cut 3 yards of beading thread. Thread the needle, using the thread double. Wax and knot the tails.

Begin and end the thread on the wrong side of the ribbon or fabric. Knot and cut the thread.

Note: For a continuous edge, work the last set of beads into the first set.

Looped Edge Stitch

1. *Pass the needle through the edge and thread 5 size 11° or 15° seed beads onto the needle.

2. To finish the edge, continue from * ¼″ away from the previous loop.

Picot Tip Edge Stitch

1. Pass the needle through the edge and thread 3–5 size 11° or 15° seed beads onto the needle.

2. *Pass the needle through the edge a short distance away and back through the last bead added.

3. Thread 2 beads onto the needle. To finish the edge, continue from *. (See the note in Beaded Edges, previous page.)

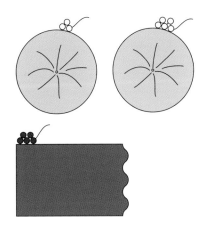

Picot Tip Edge Stitch Variation

1. Pass the needle through the edge and thread 1 size 8°, 3 size 11°, and 1 size 8° seed beads onto the needle.

2. *Pass the needle through the edge a short distance away and back through the last 2 beads added.

3. Thread 2 size 11° and 1 size 8° seed beads onto the needle. To finish the edge, continue from *. (See the note in Beaded Edges, page 72.)

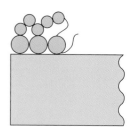

Stacked Bead Edge Stitch

1. *Pass the needle through the edge and thread 1 size 6° and 1 size 11° seed beads onto the needle. Pass the needle back through the size 6° bead and through the edge.

2. To finish the edge, continue from * ¼" away from the previous stitch.

Note: *Size 8° and 15° beads can also be used.*

Continuous Beaded Edge Stitch

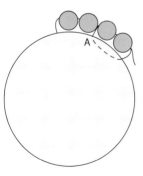

1. Pass the needle through the edge, *thread 4 size 11° seed beads onto the needle, and lay the beads flat against the fold. Pass the needle through the edge of the fabric.

2. Come up through the edge at A between the second and third beads in the row. To continue the row, follow from *. (See the note in Beaded Edges, page 72.)

Continuous Beaded Edge Stitch with Picot Tip

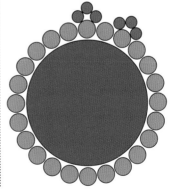

1. Follow the directions for the continuous beaded edge stitch (at left), using an even amount of beads. Do not cut the thread.

2. Follow the directions for the continuous bead stitch picot tip (page 53). Knot and cut the thread.

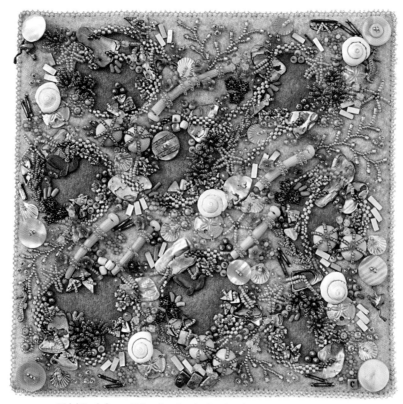

Tidal Pools (page 151), gallery inspiration for Blowing Bubbles (page 121)

Millefiori Flower Basket, project inspiration for Beaded Brooches (page 94)

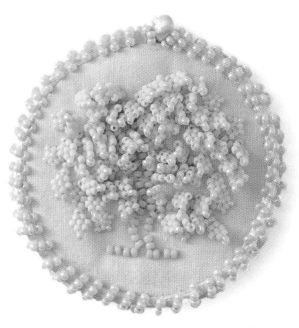

Beaded Brooches: Ash Tree project (page 94)

BEAD WOVEN STITCHES

The peyote, net, and brick stitches are called *bead woven stitches*. These stitches are formed independent from the fabric and are considered more like individual charms. In this section, you will see beads translated into realistic shapes, such as flowers, leaves, stars, and more. The peyote stitch can also be stitched directly on the fabric to form a border row or other shape.

When creating the following row(s) of the peyote stitch, the needle should pass through the beads in the previous row(s) in the same direction the row was created.

When creating the brick stitch, the rows are built across and then built up upon the previous row.

NEEDLE AND THREAD SPECIFICS

For the peyote stitches that are embroidered directly onto the fabric, cut 3 yards of beading thread, thread the needle, use the thread double, wax the thread, and knot the tails.

For the individual bead woven stitches, cut 1 yard of beading thread, thread the needle, use the thread single, and wax the thread. Start and finish each stitch with a 6″ tail of thread.

ATTACHING THE SHAPES

1. Thread both tail ends into the eye of a small sharps needle.

Note: *A bead can be added at this point if the shape is to dangle from the fabric.*

2. Stitch the needle into the fabric. Knot the threads several times.

3. To secure the position of the charm or shape, couch a tip or section in place using a single thread.

EVEN PEYOTE AND FREE-FORM PEYOTE STITCHES

Even Peyote Stitch Row

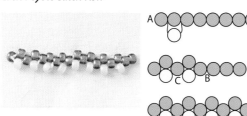

A

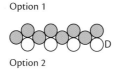

C **B**

D

Option 1

D

Option 2

1. Follow the directions for the continuous bead stitch (page 52) using the same size and color of bead.

2. Come up at **A**. Pass the needle through the first bead in the row and *thread 1 bead onto the needle. Skipping 1 bead, pass the needle through the next bead in the row.

3. Repeat from * and go down at **B**. Come up at **C** and pass through the last bead and the next bead in the row. To finish the row, continue from *, working on one side of the beginning row. Follow option 1 or 2:

Option 1: If the beginning row is an uneven number of beads, end the stitch by passing the needle through the last bead in the row. Go down at **D**. Knot the thread.

Option 2: If the beginning row is an even number of beads, pass the needle through the second-to-last bead in the row; end the stitch by adding 1 more bead onto the needle. Go down at **D**. Knot the thread.

Even Peyote Stitch Fuller Row

For a fuller row, follow the directions for the even peyote stitch row (at left) and work the stitches on the other side of the base row. Follow option 1 or 2:

Option 1: To start the next row, pass the needle through the first and second beads on the other side of the beginning row. To finish the row, continue from * in Step 2.

Option 2 (shown): To start the next row, thread 1 bead onto the needle and pass the needle through the first bead on the other side of the beginning row. To finish the row, continue from * in Step 2.

Even Peyote Stitch Row Curved

Draw a curved line with an air-erasable marking pen. Follow the directions for the continuous bead stitch curved (page 52) using 4 beads. Follow the directions for the even peyote stitch row (above), working the stitches on the outer part of the curve.

Even Peyote Stitch Multicolored Row

The beginning row of the even peyote stitch row (above left) can also be stitched with several different colors of the same size bead. Change colors every 6 beads or so. Stitch the next row following the color pattern of the beginning row.

Even Peyote Stitch Shapes

1. Use the diagram and an air-erasable marking pen to draw the shape.

2. Work the stitches in this order: even peyote stitch row (previous page), continuous bead stitch curved (page 52), and stacked bead stitch (page 64).

Basket shape with even peyote stitch, continuous bead stitch curved, and stacked bead stitch

---

Free-Form Peyote Stitch Rows

Free-form peyote stitch row

1. Follow the directions for the continuous bead stitch (page 52), using a variety of different beads and changing the size, shape, and color every 6 beads or so.

2. Follow the directions for the even peyote stitch row (previous page) or even peyote stitch fuller row (previous page). When you come to a change in bead sizes, follow option 1 or 2:

Option 1: If the next bead in the beginning row is larger, add 1 larger bead onto the needle to reach the large bead in the row.

Option 2: If the next bead in the beginning row is smaller, add 1, 2, or 3 small beads to reach the smaller bead in the row.

Free-form peyote stitch fuller row

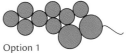

Option 1

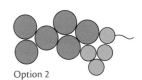

Option 2

CIRCULAR PEYOTE AND NETTED STITCHES

Center Stitch

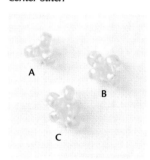

A. 3 beads, B. 4 beads, C. 5 beads

1. Thread 3, 4, or 5 beads onto the needle. Knot the thread twice to complete the circle, leaving the beginning thread 6" long.

2. Pass the needle through the beads a second time and cut the thread.

Simple Flower Stitch

A. 3 beads, B. 4 beads, C. 5 beads

1. Follow Step 1 of the center stitch (at left) with the first color bead. Pass the needle through the next bead in the first row.

2. *Thread 1 bead of a second color onto the needle. Pass the needle through the next bead in the first row. Continue from * for each remaining bead in the first row.

Note: *This second color of bead can be a smaller-size bead.*

3. Pass the needle through all the beads in the first row. Cut the thread.

Flower Stitch with Picot Tip Petals

A. 3 beads, B. 4 beads, C. 5 beads

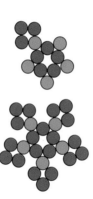

1. Follow Steps 1 and 2 of the simple flower stitch (above right) using a different color for the second row. Pass the needle through the next bead in the second row.

2. *Thread 3 beads of the first color onto the needle. Pass the needle through the next bead in the second row. Continue from * for each remaining bead in the second row.

3. Pass the needle through the next bead in the first row. Pass the needle through all the beads in the first row. Cut the thread.

Flower Stitch with Pointed Petals

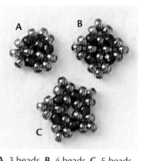

A. 3 beads, B. 4 beads, C. 5 beads

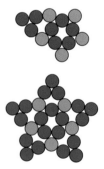

1. Follow Steps 1 and 2 of the simple flower stitch (above). Pass the needle through the next bead in the second row.

2. *Thread 3 beads of the first color onto the needle. Pass the needle through the previous bead in the second row again. Pass the needle through the next bead in the first and second row. Continue from * for each remaining bead in the second row.

3. Follow Step 3 of the flower stitch with picot tip petals (at left).

Star Stitch

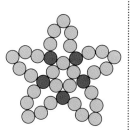

1. Follow Steps 1 and 2 of the simple flower stitch (previous page) with a 5-bead center. Pass the needle through the next bead in the second row.

2. Points: *Thread 5 beads of the first color onto the needle. Pass the needle through the next bead in the second row. Continue from * for each remaining bead in the second row.

3. Pass the needle through the first point added. Repeat for each point.

4. Follow Step 3 of the flower stitch with pointed petals (previous page).

Petite Star Stitch

1. Follow Step 1 of the center stitch (previous page) with 5 size 11° seed beads of the first color. Pass the needle through the next bead in the first row.

2. *Thread 3 size 15° seed beads onto the needle. Pass the needle through the next bead in the first row. Continue from * for each remaining bead in the first row.

3. Pass the needle through all the beads in the first row. Cut the thread.

Starfish Stitch

1. Follow Step 1 of the star stitch (above).

2. Work the points using the first color and the number of beads listed.

Point A: Thread 5 beads onto the needle. *Pass the needle through the next bead in the second row.

Point B: Thread 7 beads onto the needle. Repeat from *.

Point C: Thread 9 beads onto the needle. Repeat from *.

3. Follow Steps 3 and 4 of the star stitch (above).

Double Flower Stitch

1. Follow Steps 1–3 of the star stitch (above left). Pass the needle through the next bead in the first row.

2. *Thread 3 beads of the second color onto the needle. Pass the needle through the middle bead of the point. Thread 3 more beads onto the needle and pass the needle through the first bead in the row again.

3. Pass the needle through the next bead in the second row and the next bead in the first row. Continue from * for each remaining bead in the first row.

4. Pass the needle through all the beads in the first row. Cut the thread.

Spider Webbed Stitch

1. Use the thread double and waxed and size 11° seed beads. Thread 15 beads onto the needle. Knot together the tail twice. Pass the needle through 1 bead.

2. *Thread 5 beads onto the needle. Skip 2 beads in the beginning row, and pass the needle through the next bead in the beginning row. Repeat from *.

3. Pass the needle through the middle bead of the next point in the second row. **Thread 9 beads onto the needle. Repeat from ** for each remaining point in the second row.

4. Pass the needle through the next bead in the second row and through the first point added. Repeat this step for each point.

5. Pass the needle through the second row and to a bead in the first row. Pass the needle through all the beads in the first row. Cut the thread.

Crossed Heart Stitch

1. Use the thread double and waxed and size 11° seed beads. Thread 15 beads of color 1 and 2 beads of color 2 onto the needle. Pass the needle from left to right through the first bead of color 1. (See note below.)

2. Thread 9 beads of color 1 onto the needle. Pass the needle through the last 5 beads of color 1 from right to left in the first row. (See note below.)

3. Thread 2 beads of color 2 onto the needle. Pass the needle through the first bead of color 1. Pass the needle through all of the beads of color 1. Cut the thread.

Note: *This changes the direction of the bead.*

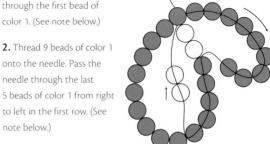

BRICK STITCHES

Basic Brick Stitch

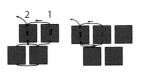

1. Starting row (SR): Thread 2 beads onto the needle and knot together the tails twice. *Pass the needle through bead 2, bead 1, and back through bead 2.

2. Increase row (IR): Thread 2 beads onto the needle and pass the needle through the loop as shown. Repeat from * and thread 1 bead onto the needle. Pass the needle through the loop and back through the bead. Continue this step for each increase row.

3. Decrease row (DR): Thread 2 beads onto the needle and pass the needle through the loop as shown. Repeat from * if more beads are added to this row. Continue this step for each decrease row.

4. Finishing: Pass the needle through the beads on one edge down to the bottom row. Cut the thread.

Basket Stitch

				Row 4 I R
				Row 3 I R
				Row 2 I R
				Row 1 SR

1. Use the thread double and waxed. Follow Steps 1 and 2 of the basic brick stitch (above).

2. Follow Step 4 of the basic brick stitch (above). Cut the thread.

Basket Stitch with Handle

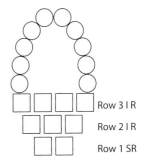

Row 3 I R
Row 2 I R
Row 1 SR

1. Follow Step 1 of the basket stitch (at left).

2. Thread enough seed beads onto the needle to make a handle and to reach the bead at the end of Row 3.

3. Pass the needle through the beads on an edge down to the bottom row. Continue through the other edge, through the handle, and down the edge again to the bottom row. Cut the thread.

Simple Leaf Stitch

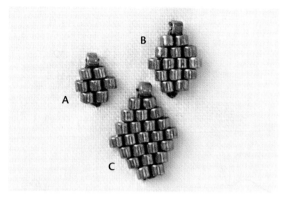

A. Small, B. Medium, C. Large

1. Follow Steps 1–3 of the basic brick stitch (page 83), using the number of beads in the small, medium, or large leaf diagrams (below).

2. Tip: Thread 1 bead onto the needle. Pass the needle through the first and second beads in the previous row, and back through the new bead.

3. Follow Step 4 of the basic brick stitch. Cut the thread.

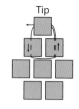

Tip

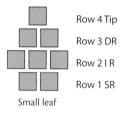

Row 4 Tip
Row 3 DR
Row 2 I R
Row 1 SR

Small leaf

Row 6 Tip
Row 5 DR
Row 4 DR
Row 3 I R
Row 2 I R
Row 1 SR

Medium leaf

Row 8 Tip
Row 7 DR
Row 6 DR
Row 5 DR
Row 4 I R
Row 3 I R
Row 2 I R
Row 1 SR

Large leaf

Grape Stitch

1. Follow Steps 1 and 2 of the simple leaf stitch (above), using the medium or large leaf diagram.

2. Pass the needle through the beads on an edge down to the bottom row, pulling the thread slightly to curve the edge.

3. Continue through the other edge, pulling the thread slightly to curve the edge. Go through the tip and down the edge again to the bottom row. Cut the thread.

Pointed Leaf Stitch

Row 5 I R
Row 4 I R
Row 3 I R
Row 2 I R
Row 1 SR

1. Follow Steps 1–3 of the basic brick stitch (page 83), using the number of beads in the bead diagram.

2. Points: Thread 3 beads onto the needle. *Pass the needle down through the next bead in the row and back up through the following bead.

3. Thread 5–7 beads onto the needle and repeat from *. Thread 3 beads onto the needle and repeat from *.

4. Pass the needle through the beads on an edge down to the bottom row, thread 1 bead onto the needle, and continue through the other edge and through a loop of the top row. Cut the thread.

PROJECT DESIGNS

Feminine Fancies (page 86)

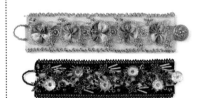

Beaded Brooches (page 94)

Spider's Webs (page 102)

Beaded Bracelets (page 108)

Scrap Roll (page 114)

Blowing Bubbles (page 121)

Beaded Tandletons (page 126)

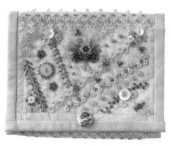

CQ Sewing Caddy (page 132)

Eight projects are included in this book, each with its own unique characteristics, style, skill level, and, of course, commitment. See Choosing a Project (page 32) for more information.

A few of the projects have two or more designs to choose from, as well as some additional examples of the project designs included for inspiration. The gallery (page 142) has even more examples of inspirational pieces, as well as other pieces made using the stitches listed in Bead Embroidery and Bead Woven Stitches (page 45).

FEMININE FANCIES

SKILL LEVEL: INTERMEDIATE TO ADVANCED

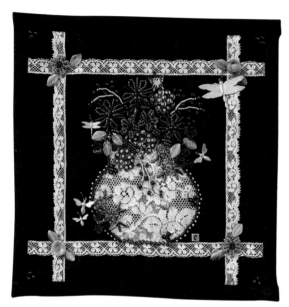

Project A: *Bouquet of Flowers; finished size: 8¼″ × 8¼″*

Project B: *Fan and Flowers; finished size: 7½″ × 7½″*

This project offers two appliqué designs—a fan and a vase—both of which are worked on a wholecloth background. Each design is worked with different pattern of bead embroidery and embellishments. These small wallhangings would fit nicely into an artist's easel— or you can add a cord hanger (page 104) so that it can be hung on the wall.

Materials

Note: Not all items listed in Materials are pictured.

- ¼ yard of fabric for base (based on 40"-wide fabric)
- ¼ yard of featherweight interfacing (such as Pellon 911FF Fusible Featherweight)
- ¼ yard of 5"-wide lace fabric
- ¼ yard of HeatnBond Lite
- 1 yard of ⅜" flat lace trim
- 1 spool of sewing thread
- 1 bobbin or card of beading thread
- Needles: small sharps and beading
- 1 package *each* of size 6° seed beads: 2 colors
- 1 package *each* of size 8° seed beads: 5 colors
- 1 package *each* of size 11° seed beads: 11 colors
- 1 package *each* of size 15° seed beads: 3 colors

For Project A

- ¼ yard of batting
- 1 package *each* of bugle beads: 2 colors
- 1 package of 5 mm sequins
- 7 charms in a variety of sizes
- 2 shank buttons, size ⅝"
- 13 leaf beads, size 12 mm × 8 mm
- 5 flower beads, size 10 mm
- 4 flower beads, size 6 mm
- 3 flower rondelles, size 4 mm

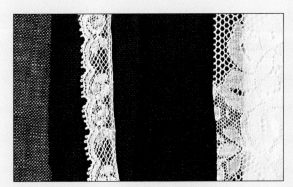

Fabric and lace

Other components

Seed and bugle beads

For Project B

- ¼ yard of fast2fuse
- 1 yard of ⅝"-wide rayon hem binding
- 1 package of bugle beads: 1 color
- 1 shank button, size ¾"
- 1 shank button, size ⅝"
- 18 leaf beads, size 12 mm × 8 mm
- 7 leaf beads, size 10 mm × 8 mm
- 12 flower beads, size 10 mm
- 17 flower beads, size 6 mm
- 15 flower rondelles, size 4 mm
- 8 flower buttons, size 6 mm

PROJECT A: BOUQUET OF FLOWERS

Cutting

From the fabric:

- 2 squares 8″ × 8″
- 2 strips 3″ × 8″
- 2 strips 3″ × 10″

From the other materials:

- 1 square of featherweight interfacing 8″ × 8″
- 1 square of batting 8″ × 8″
- 1 square of lace fabric 5″ × 5″
- 1 square of HeatnBond 5″ × 5″
- 4 pieces of lace trim, 8″ each

SEWING

1. Fuse the 8″ × 8″ piece of interfacing to the wrong side of a fabric square.

2. Measure and mark with a chalk pencil 1½″ from all 4 raw edges.

3. Pin 2 pieces of lace trim vertically, with the straight edges on the chalk line. Hand stitch in place with sewing thread.

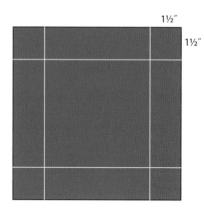

4. Pin 2 pieces of lace trim horizontally, with the straight edges on the chalk line. Hand stitch in place with sewing thread.

5. Fuse the HeatnBond to the wrong side of the lace square. Draw the vase pattern (below) on the paper side. Cut out the template and remove the paper.

6. Place the vase in the center of the square, flush with the lower horizontal piece of lace. Fuse the vase in place. Hand stitch in place with sewing thread if needed.

7. Stitch a basting stitch ¼″ in from the raw edges of the fabric base.

EMBROIDERY AND EMBELLISHMENT

See Let's Get Started! (page 36) as needed, Index of Stitches (page 157) for page numbers, and Bead Embroidery and Bead Woven Stitches (page 45) for stitch directions.

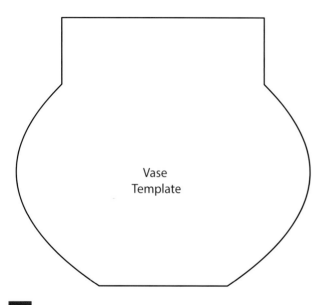

Vase
Template

Use the photograph as a reference to work the stitches in the order they are listed.

Large components		
1. Flower with lazy daisy petals		
Center, stacked bead stitch: 6° & 11° SBs	Petals, lazy daisy stitch fancy: 8° & 11° SBs	Details, single bead stitch: Bugle beads
2. Sequin rose stitch: Sequins & 11° SBs	3. Double flower stitch: 2 colors of 11° SBs	4. Center, stacked bead stitch: Flower rondelle & 11° SB
5. Button: Stitch with beading thread	6. Single bead stitch: Leaf beads	7. Grape stitch: 11° SBs, stitched on with 8° SB
Medium components		
8. Continuous bead stitch curved: 11° SBs	9. Stacked bead stitch: 8° & 11° SBs	10. Picot tip stitch: 6° SB, flower bead & 15° SBs
11. Flower with petite petals, stacked bead stitch: 6° & 11° SBs	12. Single bead stitch: Bugle bead	13. Group of 3 beaded pistil stitches: 11° & 8° SBs
Small components		
14. Picot tip stitch: Flower bead & 15° SBs	15. Group of 1–3 stacked bead stitches: 6° & 11° SBs	16. Stacked bead stitch: Flower rondelle & 15° SBs
Vase edge and details		
17. Even peyote stitch row: 2 colors of 11° SBs		18. Stacked bead stitch: 6° & 11° SBs
19. Front-to-back hole charm stitches: Charms & 11° SBs		

ASSEMBLY

1. If needed, press the embroidered front from the wrong side to remove any wrinkles in the fabric.

2. Place the other 8″ × 8″ piece of fabric right side down. Place the 8″ × 8″ piece of batting on top of the square. Place the embroidered front right side up on top of the batting.

3. Pin together the layers.

4. Fold the width of the 2 strips 3″ × 8″ in half. Press the fold.

5. Pin the raw edges of the folded 8″ strips even with the vertical edges of the layered pieces.

6. Stitch in place with a ⅜″ seam allowance.

7. Press the seam flat. Press and pin the folded edge to the backing.

8. Hand stitch the fold to the backing with sewing thread.

9. Fold the width of the 2 strips 3″ × 10″ in half. Press the fold.

10. Pin the raw edges of the folded 10″ strips even with the horizontal edges of the layered pieces.

11. Repeat Steps 6–8, tucking in and hand stitching the ends and the fold.

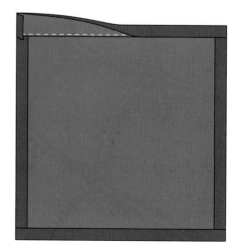

PROJECT B: FAN AND FLOWERS

Cutting

From the fabric:

- 1 square 8″ × 8″
- 1 square 7″ × 7″

From the rayon binding:

- 2 pieces 7″
- 2 pieces 9″

From the other materials:

- 1 square of featherweight interfacing 8″ × 8″
- 1 square of fast2fuse 7″ × 7″
- 1 square of lace fabric 5″ × 5″
- 1 square of HeatnBond 5″ × 5″
- 4 pieces of flat lace trim, 6″ each

SEWING

1. Fuse the 8″ × 8″ piece of interfacing to the wrong side of the 8″ × 8″ fabric square.

2. Measure and mark with a chalk pencil 3½″ from the corners on the top and bottom and 2½″ from the corners on the sides. Connect the 2 marks and draw a diagonal line across each corner.

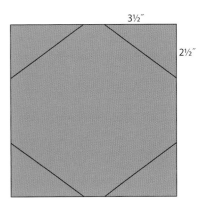

3. Pin each piece of lace trim with the straight edges along a chalk line. Hand stitch in place with sewing thread.

4. Fuse the HeatnBond to the wrong side of the lace square. Draw the fan pattern (below) on the paper side. Cut out the template and remove the paper.

5. Place the fan in the center of the square and fuse in place. Hand stitch in place with sewing thread if needed.

6. Stitch a basting stitch ¼″ in from the raw edges of the fabric base.

7. With an air-erasable marking pen, draw in the lines of the fan.

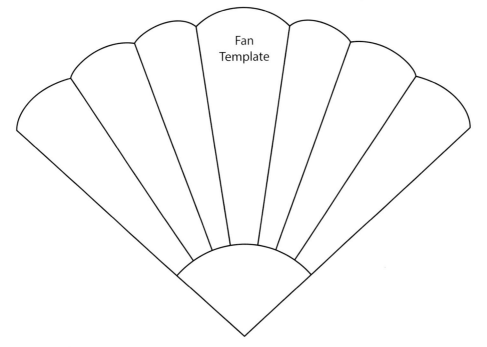

Fan Template

EMBROIDERY AND EMBELLISHMENT

See Let's Get Started! (page 36) as needed, Index of Stitches (page 157) for page numbers, and Bead Embroidery and Bead Woven Stitches (page 45) for stitch directions.

EMBROIDERY STITCH DIAGRAM *SB = seed bead*		
Fan		
1. Double bubble stitch: 8° & 11° SBs	2. Button: Stitch with beading thread	3. Continuous bead stitch curved: 11° SBs
4. Stacked bead stitch: 6° & 11° SBs	5. Stacked bead stitch: 8° & 11° SBs	6. Continuous bead stitch straight: 11° SBs
7. Bird tracks border row stitch, single bead stitch: Bugle beads	8. Beaded stamen stitch: Flower bead & 11° SBs	9. Stacked bead stitch: Flower bead & 11° SBs
Floral arrangements		
10. French rose stitch: 8°, 11° & 15° SBs	11. Small French rose stitch: 6° & 11° SBs	12. Beaded stamen stitch: Flower bead & 11° SBs
13. Stacked bead stitch: Flower bead & 15° SB	14. Stacked bead stitch: Flower rondelle & 15° SBs	15 & 16. Single bead stitch: Flower button & leaf beads
17. Top-to-bottom hole charm dangle stitch: 11° & 8° SBs, flower rondelle, leaf bead, and 8° & 15° SBs		

ASSEMBLY

1. If needed, press the embroidered front from the wrong side to remove any wrinkles in the fabric.

2. Lay the right side of the embroidered front faceup. Place the 2 pieces of 8″ rayon seam binding on the vertical raw edges of the square. Machine stitch in place.

3. Place the 2 pieces of 10″ rayon seam binding on the horizontal raw edges of the embroidered square. Machine stitch in place.

4. Fuse the wrong side of the 7″ × 7″ piece of fabric to one side of the 7″ × 7″ square of fast2fuse.

5. Place the wrong side of the embroidered front to the other side of the fast2fuse square.

6. Fold and pin the vertical raw edges of the embroidered front and seam binding square over the fabric-covered side of the fast2fuse. Hand stitch the seam binding to the fabric.

7. Fold and pin the horizontal raw edges of the embroidered front and seam binding over the fabric-covered side of the fast2fuse. Hand stitch the seam binding to the fabric.

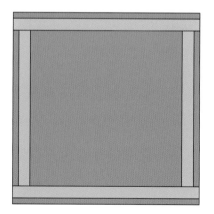

8. Stitch the outer edges with the picot tip edge stitch variation (page 74), using size 8° and 11° seed beads.

Use the photograph as a reference to work the stitches in the order they are listed.

BEADED BROOCHES

Project A: Spring in Bloom, finished size: 2⅜″ × 3½″,
skill level: beginner

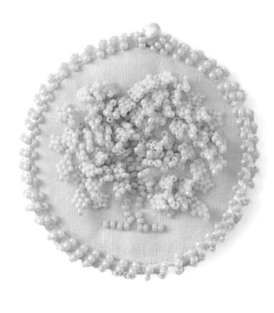

Project B: Ash Tree, finished size: 2¾″ diameter,
skill level: intermediate

These lovely little brooches are simple yet elegant and surely will be a welcome addition to any wardrobe. There are two designs to choose from, each using a slightly different group of stitches. I also included two additional ideas for inspiration.

Additional Inspiration

Brazilian Roses, finished size: 2″ diameter

Millefiori Flower Basket, finished size: 1⅞″ diameter

Basic Brooch

Note: See Project A: Spring in Bloom (page 97) or Project B: Ash Tree (page 99) for additional Materials needed for each brooch.

- ¼ yard of solid-color cotton, silk, or linen fabric (based on 40″-wide fabric)
- ¼ yard of sheer-weight interfacing (such as Pellon 906 Fusible Sheerweight)
- ⅛ yard of craft batting
- ⅛ yard of fast2fuse
- 9″ × 12″ felt square
- 1 spool of sewing thread
- Small sharps needle
- 1½″ pin back

Cutting

- 1 square of fabric 5″ × 5″
- 1 square of sheerweight interfacing 5″ × 5″
- 1 circle of batting using template B (page 100)
- 1 circle of fast2fuse using template B (page 100)
- 1 circle of felt using template B (page 100)

CREATING THE FABRIC BASE

1. Fuse the 5″ × 5″ interfacing square to the wrong side of the 5″ × 5″ fabric square.

2. Cut a circle of interfaced fabric using template A (page 100). Apply a thin line of Fray Check along the raw edges of the fabric.

3. Trim ⅛″ off the circle of batting. Glue the batting to the fast2fuse with tacky glue.

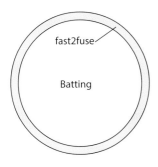

4. Thread a small sharps needle with sewing thread and knot the tails.

5. Tackstitch the thread ¼″ from the fabric's raw edge. Stitch a basting stitch around the outer circle of fabric ¼″ from the raw edge.

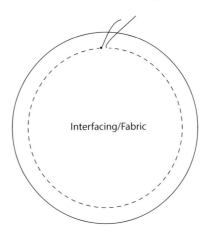

6. Place the batting side of the fast2fuse circle next to the interfacing side of the fabric circle. Pull the thread to gather the stitches and form the fabric around the fast2fuse edge. Tackstitch, knot, and cut the thread.

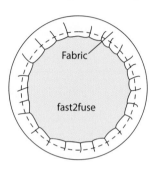

7. Press the front of the base. Press the back of the base, being careful to press only the fabric without touching the fast2fuse.

8. Refer to Directions in Project A: Spring in Bloom (next page) or Directions in Project B: Ash Tree (page 99) to complete the fabric base; then move on to Embroidery and Embellishment.

EMBROIDERY AND EMBELLISHMENT

See Let's Get Started! (page 36) as needed, Index of Stitches (page 157) for page numbers, and Bead Embroidery and Bead Woven Stitches (page 45) for stitch directions.

See Project A: Spring in Bloom (next page) or Project B: Ash Tree (page 99) for embroidery and embellishment for each project.

FINISHING THE FABRIC BASE

1. After you have added the embroidery and embellishment for Project A (next page) or Project B (page 99), place the pin back on the felt and make a mark at each end. Clip into the felt at each mark.

2. Open the pin back and insert it into the felt at the clips. Hand stitch the bar to the felt with sewing thread.

3. Place a line of tacky glue around the outer edge of the back of the felt; place this on the back of the embroidered brooch.

PROJECT A: SPRING IN BLOOM

Use the photograph as a reference to work the stitches in the order they are listed.

Materials

- 1 fabric base (from Creating the Fabric Base, page 95)
- 4" of ⅜" flat lace trim
- 1 package *each* of size 8° seed beads: 4 colors
- 1 package *each* of size 11° seed beads: 5 colors
- 3 oval buttons, size ⅜"
- 3 flower beads, size 8 mm
- 4 butterfly beads, size 4 mm
- 3 tulip beads, size 6 mm × 8 mm
- 3 round beads, size 4 mm
- 3 rondelles, size 4 mm
- 1 bobbin or card of beading thread
- Beading needle

Seed beads   Fabric

DIRECTIONS

1. Follow the directions for Creating the Fabric Base (page 95).

2. Mark a line ¾" up from the edge of the front of the base. Use sewing thread to hand stitch the lace in place along this line.

Other components

EMBROIDERY STITCH DIAGRAM	*SB = seed bead*

1. Button hole decoration stitches: 11° SBs	2. Stacked bead stitch: 8° & 11° SBs	3. Continuous bead stitch: 11° SBs
4. Stacked bead stitch: 8° SB, flower bead & 11° SB	5. Stacked bead stitch group: 8° & 11° SBs	6. Single bead stitch: Butterfly bead	7. Single bead stitch: 11° SBs

Finishing touches

8. Stacked bead edge stitch: 8° & 11° SBs

9. Top-to-bottom hole charm dangle stitch: 11° & 8° SBs, 4 mm round bead, rondelle, tulip bead & 11° SBs

3. Follow the directions for Finishing the Fabric Base (page 96).

PROJECT B: ASH TREE

Materials

- 1 fabric base (from Creating the Fabric Base, page 95)
- 1 package *each* of size 11° seed beads: 2 colors
- 1 package *each* of size 15° seed beads: 2 colors
- 1 package of size 11° delica beads: 1 color
- 12" rattail cord
- 1 bobbin or card of beading thread
- Beading needle

Fabric   Seed and delica beads

DIRECTIONS

1. Follow the directions for Creating the Fabric Base (page 95).

2. Use the tree diagram (below) and an air-erasable marking pen to draw the tree shape.

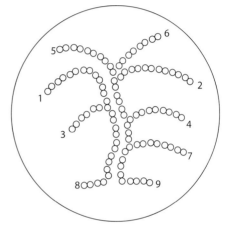

Use the diagram as a reference to work the trunk and branches stitches in the order they are listed.

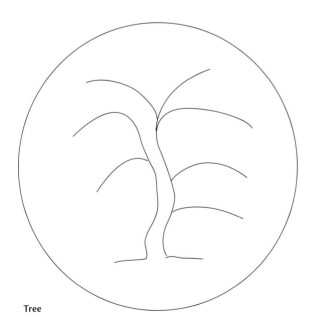

Tree

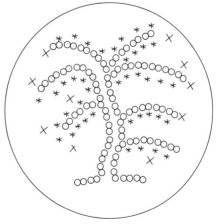

Use the diagram as a reference to work the flower and leaf stitches, shown with crosses and stars.

Trunk	Branches	Flowers (X)		Leaves (*)
1 & 2. Grouped bead stitch: 11° SBs	3–9. Grouped bead stitch: 11° SBs	Simple flower stitch: 2 colors of 15° SBs	Single bead stitch: 15° SB	Simple leaf stitch—small: 11° delica beads

3. Flowers: Stitch the tail down at an **X**. Stitch a bead in the center of the flower. Knot and cut the thread.

4. Leaves: Thread the tails with a size 11° seed bead; then stitch down at an •. Knot and cut the thread.

5. Follow the directions for Cord with Looped Edge Stitch (at right).

6. Follow the directions for Finishing the Fabric Base (page 96).

Cord with Looped Edge Stitch

1. Measure the edge of the base, add 4″, and cut the cord. Hand stitch one end on the wrong side, 2″ down from the edge.

2. With beading thread, *pass the needle through the wrong side of the fabric just under the cord. Thread with 5–7 size 11° seed beads onto the needle.

Note: *When the cord is flat against the fabric, as in Spider's Webs (page 102), come up on one side of the cord, thread the beads on the needle, and pass the needle down on the other side of the cord.*

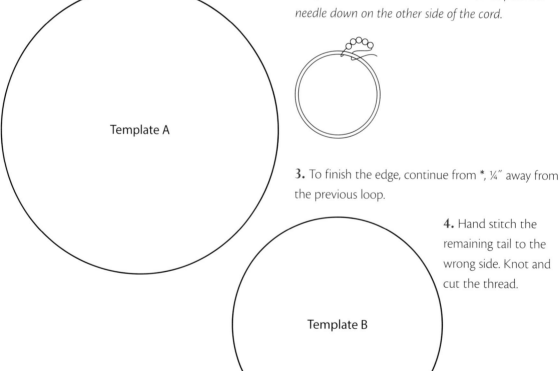

3. To finish the edge, continue from *, ¼″ away from the previous loop.

4. Hand stitch the remaining tail to the wrong side. Knot and cut the thread.

Template A

Template B

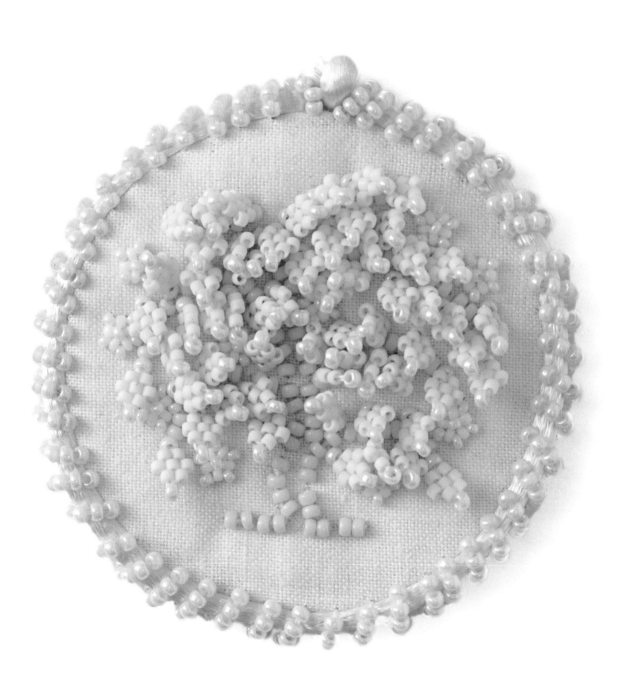

SPIDER'S WEBS

Spiders Hide in the Dusk, finished size: 9″ × 9″

This project begins with a wholecloth base that is machine quilted. The base is then stitched to a firm stabilizer. The webs, spiders, and button flowers are worked in bead embroidery stitches.

Additional Inspiration

In this version, the web is larger and stitched with the free-form peyote stitch rows. I added bead woven components such as the simple flower and pointed leaf stitch.

Along Came a Spider, finished size: 9″ × 9″

Materials

Note: Not all items listed in Materials are pictured.

- ½ yard of fabric for base (based on 40"-wide fabric)
- ½ yard of batting
- 9" × 12" felt square

Seed and bugle beads

- ¼ yard of fast2fuse
- 2½ yards of rattail cord
- 1 spool of decorative sewing thread
- 1 spool of sewing thread
- 1 ball of perle cotton #8
- 2 bobbins or cards of beading thread
- Needles: Small sharps, cotton darner, and beading
- 1 package *each* of size 6° seed beads: 4 colors
- 1 package *each* of size 8° seed beads: 5 colors
- 1 package *each* of size 11° seed beads: 9 colors
- 1 package of size 15° seed beads: 1 color
- 1 package *each* of bugle beads: 2 colors
- 4 glass buttons (shank or sew through), size ½"
- 1 glass button (shank or sew through), size ⅝"

- 13 sew-through shell buttons, size ⅝"–¾"
- 2 sew-through buttons, size ½", for large spiders
- 2 sew-through buttons, size ⅜", for large spiders
- 1 sew-through button, size ⅜", for small spider
- 1 sew-through button, size ¼", for small spider
- 5 glass tulip beads, size 8 mm × 12 mm
- 10 glass leaf beads, size 12 mm × 8 mm
- 5 butterfly charms, size 12 mm × 12 mm

Cutting

- 1 square of fabric 14" × 14"
- 1 square of batting 16" × 16"
- 1 square of fast2fuse 9" × 9"
- 1 square of felt 9" × 9"

Fabric, cord

Other components

SEWING

1. Place the wrong side of the fabric square on top of the batting. Pin in place.

2. Follow the directions for Free-Form Stitching (page 40), using decorative thread on the fabric and batting sandwich.

3. Trim the fabric sandwich to 12″ × 12″. Machine stitch a basting stitch ¼″ from the raw edges.

4. Place the batting side of the fabric sandwich onto the 9″ × 9″ piece of fast2fuse.

5. Fold and pin the vertical raw edges of the fabric sandwich over the edges of the fast2fuse.

6. Hand stitch the raw edges of the fabric sandwich to the fast2fuse with sewing thread.

7. Fold and pin the horizontal raw edges of the fabric sandwich over the edges of the fast2fuse. Repeat Step 6.

EMBROIDERY AND EMBELLISHMENT

See Let's Get Started! (page 36) as needed, Index of Stitches (page 157) for page numbers, and Bead Embroidery and Bead Woven Stitches (page 45) for stitch directions.

Couched Cord Border

1. Make a knot at the beginning end of the rattail cord. Knot the cord every 3″ or so.

2. Refer to the photograph (page 107) for placement. Hold or pin the cord in place.

3. Couch the cord every ¼″ or so with perle cotton.

4. Knot the end of the cord. Cut off the excess cord, and treat both ends with Fray Check. Knot and cut the thread.

Cord Hanger and Backing

1. Cut a piece of rattail cord 8″. Fold in half and knot the tails together.

2. Pin the knot in the center of the top edge on the wrong side of the base, with the loop facing up; hand stitch this to the wrong side of the base with perle cotton. Knot and cut the thread.

3. Pin the 9″ × 9″ felt square to the wrong side of the base. Hand stitch in place with sewing thread. Knot and cut the thread.

Spiderwebs

Using an air-erasable pen, draw in the lines of the spiderwebs, using the diagrams (below) as a guide. Stitch the spokes first and then the connecting bars in the order they are listed. Refer to the photograph (page 107) for placement.

Note: Some spokes are shorter than others, so not all of the pattern will be needed. In addition, you may have to stop and restart a spoke or connecting bar to fit around the couched cord border.

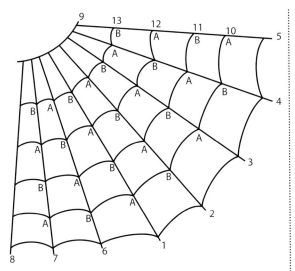

Large spiderweb: Enlarge 200%.

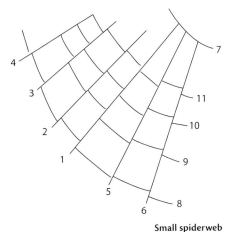

Small spiderweb

SB = seed bead

Spokes: 1, 2, 3, 4, 5, 6, 7 & 8

Continuous bead stitch straight, 6 SBs in each size & color:
11°, 8°, 11°, 8°, 11°, 8°, 11°, 8°, 11°, 8°, 11°

Connecting bars: 9, 10, 11, 12 & 13

Continuous bead stitch curved: 6 SBs 11°

Details

A. Stacked bead stitch:
6° & 11° SBs

B. Bead combination stitch:
11° SBs & bugle beads

Note: Work the rows in order from 1 to 8, then 9, and 10 to 13. Stitch in the remaining components.

SB = seed bead

Spokes: 1, 2, 3, 4, 5 & 6

Continuous bead stitch straight, 6 SBs 11° in each color

Connecting Bar: 7

Continuous bead stitch curved: 6 SBs 11°

Connecting bars: 8, 9, 10 & 11

Bead combination stitch: 11° SBs & bugle beads
(Add more or subtract the 11° SBs to fit the pattern.)

Note: Work the rows in order from 1 to 6, then 7, and 8 to 11.

Stitch the 13 sew-through shell buttons in sizes ⅝"–¾" with perle cotton. Refer to the photograph (page 107) for placement.

BUTTON EMBROIDERY STITCH DIAGRAM   *SB = seed bead*

Buttons: 1–13		
Button hole decoration stitches, grouped bead stitch: 11° SBs		
Buttons: 1, 2, 3, 4, 5, 7, 8, 10 & 11	Buttons: 1, 4, 7, 10 & 11	Buttons: 3, 5 & 8
Continuous bead stitch straight: 11° SBs	Single bead stitch: Leaf bead	Stacked bead stitch: 6° & 11° SBs
Flower petals		
Buttons: 1, 7 & 13	Buttons: 2 & 9	Buttons: 3 & 8
Stacked bead stitch: 6° & 11° SBs	Bead combination stitch: 11° SBs & bugle beads	Bead cascade stitch: 6° & 11° SBs
Buttons 4 and 12	**Buttons 5 and 10**	**Buttons 6 and 11**
Button bezel stitch: 11° SBs Stacked bead stitch: 8° & 15° SBs	Bead combination stitch: 11° & 8° SBs	Lazy daisy stitch fancy: 8° & 11° SBs

ADDITIONAL DETAILS   *SB = seed bead*

14. Cord with looped edge stitch*: 11° SBs	15. Glass buttons: Grouped bead stitch or stitch with perle cotton		16. Picot tip stitch: Tulip bead & 11° SBs
17. Spider stitch: Buttons and 11° & 15° SBs	18. Continuous bead stitch: 11° SBs	19. Group of 3 stacked bead stitches: 6° & 11° SBs	20. Front-to-back hole charm stitch: Butterfly charms & 11° SBs

Note: See the note in Cord with Looped Edge Stitch (page 100) for the looped edge stitch.

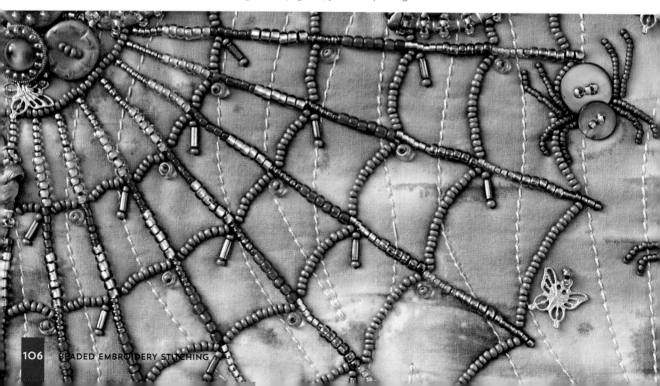

Use the photograph as a reference to work the stitches in the order they are listed.

BEADED BRACELETS

Project A: Summer Blooms, finished size: 7½" × 1¾", skill level: Beginner to intermediate

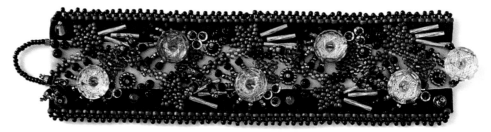

Project B: The Stars Are Out Tonight, finished size: 7½" × 1¾", skill level: intermediate to advanced

These beautiful wrist adornments provide the perfect backdrop to display your beads, buttons, and charms using a variety of bead embroidery and bead woven stitches. There are two designs to choose from, as well as some additional inspiration examples, each using a slightly different group of stitches and materials.

Additional Inspiration

Glass Flowers, finished size: 7½" × 1½"

The Shore, finished size: 8" × 1⅞"

This is a simpler version of the **Summer Blooms** bracelet, replacing the rosettes with glass flowers.

This is a version of the **Stars Are Out Tonight** bracelet, incorporating glass and shell beads with bead woven components.

Basic Bracelet

Note: *See Project A: Summer Blooms (page 111) or Project B: The Stars Are Out Tonight (page 112) for additional Materials needed for each bracelet.*

- 1 yard of grosgrain or jacquard ribbon, 1″–2″ wide
- 1 yard of ribbon or flat lace trim in a narrower width
- ½ yard of midweight fusible interfacing (such as Pellon 931TD Fusible Midweight)
- 1 spool of sewing thread
- Small sharps needle

CREATING THE RIBBON BASE

1. Measure your wrist with the ribbon, double it, and add ½″ to this measurement. Cut the ribbon. *Note:* This should be a comfortable length—not too tight.

2. Cut the second ribbon or piece of lace the same length as the first ribbon.

3. With a glue stick, draw a line down the center of the ribbon width.

4. Lay the second ribbon or piece of lace along this line. Pin in place if needed. Thread the needle with sewing thread and stitch the ribbon or lace in place with a straight stitch or whipstitch.

5. Place a line of Fray Check along the raw edges of the 2 ribbons or the ribbon and lace. Set this aside to dry.

6. Fold the ribbon in half with right sides together; pin together the raw edges.

7. Thread the needle with sewing thread, double the thread, and knot together the tails.

8. Knot the thread into the selvage edges of the ribbon, ¼″ in from the raw edges. Stitch the seam allowance, using short straight stitches or a backstitch. Knot and cut the thread.

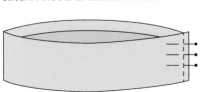

9. Still working with the wrong side out, fold the ribbon so that the seam is in the center of the length. Press the seam open.

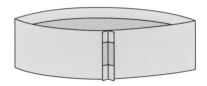

10. Turn the ribbon right side out. Press the folded edges of the bracelet flat.

11. Measure the length of the ribbon from fold to fold. Cut the interfacing this length by ⅛″ narrower than the width of the ribbon.

12. Fuse the interfacing in place on the inside of the front of the bracelet, following the manufacturer's directions.

13. Refer to Directions in Project A: Summer Blooms (page 111) or Directions in Project B: The Stars Are Out Tonight (page 112) to complete the ribbon base; then move on to Embroidery and Embellishment.

EMBROIDERY AND EMBELLISHMENT

See Let's Get Started! (page 36) as needed, Index of Stitches (page 157) for page numbers, and Bead Embroidery and Bead Woven Stitches (page 45) for stitch directions.

See Project A: Summer Blooms (next page) or Project B: The Stars Are Out Tonight (page 112) for embroidery and embellishment for each project.

FINISHING THE RIBBON BASE

1. After you have added the embroidery and embellishment for Project A (next page) or Project B (page 112), *thread the beading needle with 2 yards of beading thread, double the thread, wax it, and knot the ends together.

2. At an end of the bracelet, fold the width of the ribbon in half. Place a pin at the fold.

3. From the wrong side, stitch the needle up through the ribbon ¼" from the pin through the folded edge of the ribbon. Knot the thread.

4. Thread onto the needle 3–5 size 11° seed beads, a button, and the same number of size 11° seed beads. Stitch the needle down through the ribbon ¼" from the pin, through the folded edge of the ribbon. Knot the thread.

5. Pass the needle back through the beads, button, and beads again. Knot the thread. Repeat this step.

6. At the opposite end of the bracelet, repeat Steps 2 and 3.

7. Thread 20 or more size 11° seed beads onto the needle. Stitch the needle down through the ribbon ¼" from the fold.

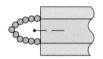 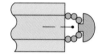

8. Test the length of the loop to make sure that it easily fits over the button and that it fits your wrist. Add or subtract beads as needed. Knot the thread.

9. Pass the needle back through the beads. Knot the thread. Repeat this step.

10. Pin together the selvage edges of one side of the bracelet sandwich.

11. Repeat Step 1. *From the wrong side, stitch the needle up through the ribbon to the selvage edge next to the fold. Follow the directions under Finishing Touches for the beaded edge stitches listed for Project A or Project B.

PROJECT A: SUMMER BLOOMS

Materials

- 1 ribbon base (from Creating the Ribbon Base, page 109)
- 1 yard of ⅜″-wide grosgrain ribbon
- 1 package of size 6° seed beads: 1 color
- 1 package of size 8° seed beads: 1 color
- 1 package *each* of size 11° seed beads: 4 colors
- 1 shank button, size ¾″, for closure
- 30 flower rondelles, size 5 mm
- 5 tulip beads, size 4 mm × 5 mm
- 10 leaf charms, size 12 mm × 8 mm
- 1 bobbin or card of beading thread
- Beading needle

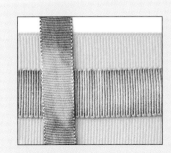

Grosgrain ribbons

Other components

Seed beads

DIRECTIONS

1. Follow the directions for Creating the Ribbon Base (page 109).

2. Cut 5 lengths of ribbon 3″ long. Follow the directions in Scrap Roll, Rosette (page 116).

3. Follow the directions for the picot tip edge stitch (page 73) using size 11° seed beads.

4. Evenly space the rosettes across the length of the bracelet. With sewing thread, hand stitch the center of each rosette to the ribbon base. Knot and cut the thread.

EMBROIDERY STITCH DIAGRAM	SB = seed bead

Large components	
1. Stem & flower stitch: 11° SBs & tulip bead	2. Floret stitch: 6° & 11° SBs

Medium and small components	
3. Front-to-back hole charm stitch, bead cascade stitch: Leaf charm & 11° SBs	4. Stacked bead stitch: 8° SB, flower rondelle & 11° SB

Finishing touches
Follow the directions for Finishing the Ribbon Base (previous page).

5. Looped edge stitch: 11° SBs

Use the photograph as a reference to work the stitches in the order they are listed.

PROJECT B: THE STARS ARE OUT TONIGHT

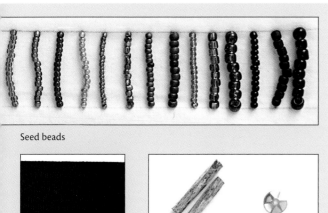

Seed beads

Ribbons

Other components

Materials

- 1 ribbon base (from Creating the Ribbon Base, page 109)
- 1 package *each* of size 6° seed beads: 2 colors
- 1 package *each* of size 8° seed beads: 3 colors
- 1 package *each* of size 11° seed beads: 8 colors
- 1 package of size 15° seed beads: 1 color
- 1 package of bugle beads: 1 color
- 6 shank buttons, size ½" (1 for closure)
- 3 round beads, size 6 mm
- 2 rondelles (open center), size 6 mm
- 15 round beads, size 4 mm
- 15 sequins
- 1 bobbin or card of beading thread
- Beading needle

DIRECTIONS

1. Follow the directions for Creating the Ribbon Base (page 109).

2. Use the stitch design diagram and an air-erasable marking pen to draw the stitch design, repeating the curves as needed.

Stitch design

3. Follow the directions for the even peyote stitch row curved (page 78) and even peyote stitch multicolored row (page 78), using 4 colors of size 11° seed beads.

4. Stagger and space the 5 buttons, size ½", evenly across the length of the bracelet. Stitch in place with sewing or beading thread.

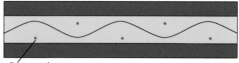

Button placement

Embroidery design and button placement

Use the photograph as a reference to work the stitches in the order they are listed.

EMBROIDERY STITCH DIAGRAM   *SB = seed bead*

Large components		
1. Star stitch: 2 colors of 11° SBs	2. Star stitch: 2 colors of 11° SBs	3. Bead combination stitch: 11° & 8° SBs (Vary the lengths.)

Medium components		
4. Single bead stitch: Bugle beads	5. Floret stitch: 6° & 15° SBs	6. Group of 3 beaded pistil stitches: 11° SBs, sequin, 4 mm round bead & 15° SBs

Small components			
7. Group of 3 stacked bead stitches: 6° & 11° SBs	8. Group of 3 stacked bead stitches: Sequin & 11° SB	9. Stacked bead stitch: 6 mm round bead & 11° SB	10. Stacked bead stitch: 6 mm rondelle and 6° & 11° SBs

Finishing touches
Follow the directions for Finishing the Ribbon Base (page 110).

11. Picot tip edge stitch variation: 8° & 11° SBs

SCRAP ROLL

SKILL LEVEL: INTERMEDIATE TO ADVANCED

Ivory and Lace, finished
size: 3½″ × 3″ (closed)
or 3½″ × 24″ (open)

This delightful roll embraces all things feminine. The base is comprised of collaged scraps and bits of lace, hankies, appliqués, ribbons, buttons, beads, and more. This project is embellished with both bead embroidery and bead woven stitches.

Additional Inspiration

Pansies and Sunflowers,
finished size: 3½″ × 3″ × 32″

In this version of the project, I used color as the main theme. I included quite a few appliqués, buttons, and large objects to embellish the base, along with the bead embroidery stitches.

Materials

Seed beads

Laces, trims, rosette, and yo-yo

Other components

Note: Not all items listed in Materials are pictured.

Foundation

- 1 wooden spool 3″ long with 2″ center
- Foundation for base: 1 yard of 2″-wide ribbon
- Lining for base: 1 yard of 2″-wide flat lace
- Fabric for base: Bits and scraps, enough to cover the 1-yard ribbon base
- Additional surface decoration for base: Bits of lace, hankies, and appliqués
- ⅛ yard of fast2fuse
- ⅛ yard of craft batting
- 2 yards of ⅜″-wide satin ribbon
- ¼ yard of flat lace
- 6 flower appliqués
- Small amount of fabric to make yo-yos for spool cover
- 12″ of rattail cord for spool cover
- Paint and brush to paint wooden spool (*optional*)
- 1 spool of sewing thread
- 2 bobbins or cards of beading thread
- 1 spool of perle cotton #8
- Needles: Small sharps, beading, and cotton darner

Beads and Embellishments

- 1 package *each* of size 6° seed beads: 3 colors
- 1 package *each* of size 8° seed beads: 5 colors
- 1 package *each* of size 11° seed beads: 5 colors
- 1 package *each* of size 15° seed beads: 2 colors
- 1 package of size 10° delica beads: 1 color
- 1 shell butterfly charm, size 10 mm × 13 mm
- 7 shell buttons (shank or sew through), size ⅜″
- 8 glass flower beads, size 7 mm × 8 mm
- 19 glass leaf beads, size 10 mm × 8 mm
- 4 shell flower beads, size 10 mm
- 31 glass flower rondelles, size 8 mm
- 2 potato pearls, size 6 mm
- 10 round beads, size 4 mm
- 9 round beads, size 3 mm
- 10 sequins, size 4 mm
- 30 freshwater pearls, size 4 mm–8 mm
- 7 mother-of-pearl buttons, size ⅜″
- 1 button, size ¾″, for closure
- 1 button, size ¾″, for spool top

Cutting

From the fabric:

- 10 circles 2″ for the yo-yos
- 1 circle ¾″ larger than fast2fuse circle (see below)
- Other bits and scraps cut 2″ × 1″–3″ (Assemble these into piles.)

From the satin ribbon:

- 1-yard length for the ties
- 5 pieces 3″ for the rosettes

From the other materials:

- 1 piece of 2″-wide ribbon 18″–27″ long for the foundation
- 1 piece of 2″-wide flat lace 1″ longer than the ribbon
- Other bits and scraps of lace or trim, 2″ × 1″–3″ (Assemble these into piles.)
- 2 pieces of lace the same length and width as the spool lip
- 1 circle *each* of fast2fuse and batting the same size as the spool top

FABRIC YO-YOS

1. Thread a small sharps needle with sewing thread. Knot the tails together. With the wrong side of the fabric facing up, fold over an ⅛" seam. Insert the needle under the seam and through the fold.

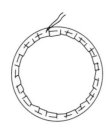

2. Gather stitch close to the folded edge through both layers of fabric. End the stitching on the right side of the fabric, but do not overlap the first gather stitch taken.

3. Pull the thread to gather the stitches tightly; anchor knot the thread into a fold of fabric. Bury the needle through the center of the fabric; knot and cut the thread.

ROSETTE

Note: When using a synthetic ribbon, sear the raw edges with a Thread Zap II pen to avoid any fraying.

1. Fold the ribbon piece in half lengthwise, right sides together, matching the raw edges. Stitch together the raw edges with sewing thread and

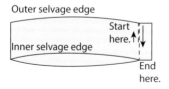

a ⅛" seam allowance. Start in the middle of the seam, working toward the outer selvage edge and then back down to the inner selvage edge. Anchor knot the thread into the selvage edges.

2. Starting at the inner selvage edge next to the seam, gather stitch through 1 layer of ribbon

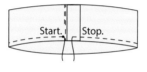

along the continuous selvage edge back to the seam.

3. Gently pull the thread to gather the stitches and form the middle of the flower. Anchor knot the thread into the raw edges.

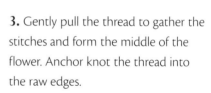

SEWING

1. Place the 2″ × 18″–27″ ribbon faceup. Draw a line 3″ in from the left end across the width of the ribbon.

2. Place a piece of paper onto the work surface. Starting at the drawn line, spray the length of ribbon with Sulky KK 2000.

3. Place a scrap of fabric or hanky at the drawn line. Overlap the right raw edge with the next scrap. Continue to collage the ribbon with the bits and scraps of fabric and hankies.

4. Hand stitch along the length of the outer edges of ribbon with sewing thread. Flip the ribbon over to the wrong side. Trim off any excess bits, if needed.

5. Place the trims and appliqués across the collaged ribbon in straight, angled, or curved lines. Hand stitch in place.

6. Make 10 fabric yo-yos (previous page) from the 2″ circles. Stitch the edges with the picot tip edge stitch (page 73), using 2 colors of size 11° seed beads.

7. Make 5 rosettes (previous page) from the ⅜″ × 3″ pieces of satin ribbon. Stitch the edges with the looped edge stitch (page 72), using size 15° seed beads.

8. Spool top: Follow the directions for Beaded Brooches, Creating the Fabric Base (page 95), using the fast2fuse, batting, and piece of fabric.

EMBROIDERY AND EMBELLISHMENT

See Let's Get Started! (page 36) as needed, Index of Stitches (page 157) for page numbers, and Bead Embroidery and Bead Woven Stitches (page 45) for stitch directions.

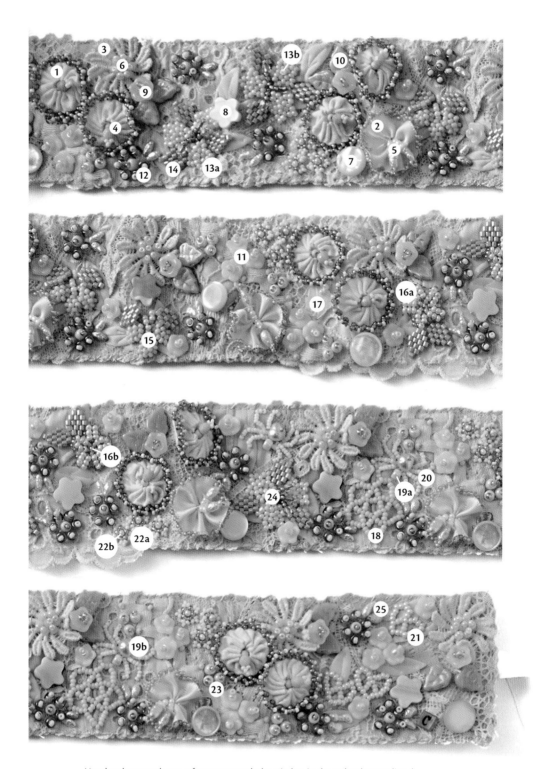

Use the photograph as a reference to work the stitches in the order they are listed.

Large components			
1. Fabric yo-yo: Stitch in place with sewing thread.	2. Rosette: Stitch in place with sewing thread.	3. Appliqués: Stitch with sewing thread.	4. Beaded pistil stitch: 8° SB, 4 mm round bead & 15° SBs
5. Beaded pistil stitch: 11° SBs, sequin, freshwater pearl & 15° SBs	6. Flower with petite petals, stacked bead stitch: 8° & 11° SBs	7. Mother-of-pearl button: Hand stitch with sewing thread or perle cotton.	8. Single bead stitch: Shell flower bead

Medium components			
9. Picot tip stitch: Tulip bead & 11° SBs	10. Single bead stitch: Leaf bead	11. Stacked bead stitch: Flower rondelle and 8° & 11° SBs	12. Flower with petite petals stacked bead stitch: 6° & 11° SBs
13a. Flower stitch with pointed petals: 2 colors of 11° SBs	13b. Center, single bead stitch: 11° SB	14. Simple leaf stitch— medium: 10° delica beads	15. Grape stitch: 11° SBs
16a. Double flower stitch: 2 colors of 11° SBs	16b. Center, single bead stitch: 11° SB	17. Front-to-back hole charm stitch: Butterfly charm & 15° SBs	18. Spider webbed stitch: 11° SBs
19a. Spider head, single bead stitch: 6° SB	19b. Spider body, stacked bead stitch: 1 pearl & 15° SB	20. Spider stitch, legs only: 15° SBs	21. Crossed heart stitch: 2 colors of 11° SBs
22a. Flower stitch with picot tip petals: 11° & 15° SBs		22b. Center, single bead stitch: 11° SB	

Small components		
23. Group of 3 stacked bead stitches: 6° & 11° SBs	24. Group of 3 beaded pistil stitches: 8° SBs, 3 mm round bead & 15° SB	25. Single bead stitch: Freshwater pearls

Use the photograph as a reference guide to work the stitches in the order they are listed.

SPOOL TOP   *SB = seed bead*

1. Button: Stitch with sewing or beading thread.	2. Flower stitch with pointed petals: See 13a and 13b (above).	3. Single bead stitch: Leaf bead

4. Cord with looped edge stitch: Rayon cord & 11° SBs

ASSEMBLY

1. Place the 2″-wide flat lace right side down. Place the ribbon base on top of the lace right side up, matching the left ends.

2. Pin together the ribbon and lace, working from left to right and stopping 5″ from the right end.

3. Fold the raw edges of the lace under ½″, flush with the right end of the collaged ribbon base.

4. Fold the width of the raw edge of the ribbon base in half, right sides together. Place a mark along this fold on the wrong side of the ribbon base to mark the center.

5. Fold the 1-yard length of ribbon in half; center and pin the fold ½″ in from the raw edge. Use sewing thread to hand stitch the fold of the ribbon to the wrong side of the ribbon base.

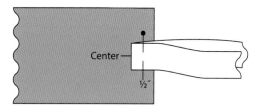

6. Pin together the right ends.

7. Whipstitch the raw edges of the ribbon base to the lace with perle cotton.

8. Hand stitch the large button to the lace with sewing thread or perle cotton, ½″ in from the end with the ribbon closure.

Wooden Spool and Base Assembly

1. Paint the wooden spool, if desired.

2. With tacky glue, glue in place the 2 pieces of lace the same size as the spool lip.

3. Lay the collaged ribbon base faceup.

4. Place a line of glue on the neck of the wooden spool and lay the left end of the ribbon base onto the line of glue. Let dry.

5. Roll the spool to wrap the 3″ of unembellished ribbon around the spool, with the lace showing. Stop at the 3″ marked line, and place a line of glue onto the ribbon base on this line. Roll the ribbon to meet this line. Let dry.

6. Glue the wrong side of the embroidered fabric circle to the top of the wooden spool.

BLOWING BUBBLES

SKILL LEVEL: INTERMEDIATE

Jewel Bubbles, finished size: 8½″ × 8½″

This colorful project begins with several squares of felt, which are used to create the reverse appliqué design for the base. The bead embroidery and embellishments follow the edges of the circle shapes and open spaces.

Additional Inspiration

In this version of the project, I used a printed felt square as the base and embroidered on and around the design. This version is a wallhanging; I added pieces of felt to create a frame around the center square.

Cogs and Gears, finished size: 9¼″ × 9¼″

Materials

- 2 felt squares 9″ × 12″ in 1 color (C1)
- 2 felt squares in 2 colors (C2 and C3)
- 1 printed felt square 9″ × 12″ (CP)
- ¼ yard of featherweight fusible interfacing (such as Pellon 911FF Fusible Featherweight)
- Circle template or circular objects for appliqué shapes
- 1 package of stuffing
- 1 spool of sewing thread
- 1 bobbin or card of beading thread
- 1 ball of perle cotton #8
- Needles: Small sharps, beading, and cotton darner
- 1 package *each* of size 6° seed beads: 4 colors
- 1 package *each* of size 8° seed beads: 5 colors
- 1 package *each* of size 11° seed beads: 5 colors
- 1 package *each* of sequins: 5 colors
- 9 buttons, size ¾″ (large)
- 15 buttons, size ⅝″ (medium)
- 17 buttons, size ½″ (small)

Cutting

From the C2 felt:

- 1 square 2¼″ × 2¼″
- 2 squares 1¾″ × 1¾″

From the C3 felt:

- 2 squares 2″ × 2″
- 2 squares 1¾″ × 1¾″

From the other materials:

- 2 squares of C1 felt 9″ × 9″ (front base and back)
- 1 square of CP felt 8⅞″ × 8⅞″
- 1 square of featherweight interfacing 8⅞″ × 8⅞″

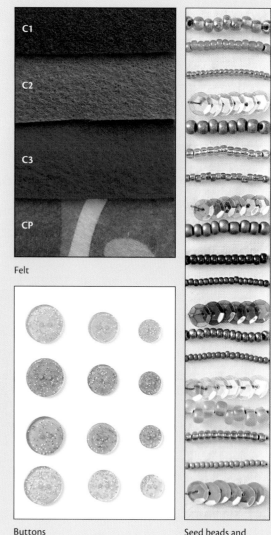

Felt

Buttons

Seed beads and sequins

SEWING

1. Referring to the circle 1 diagram, draw the circle shapes onto the C1 front base, using a chalk pencil and circle template.

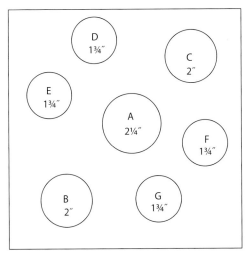

Circle 1

2. Make a small clip into the drawn line of a circle to begin cutting through the felt. Carefully cut out each circle.

3. Spray the wrong side of the C1 front base with Sulky KK 2000. Place this on top of the right side of the printed felt square.

4. Use sewing thread to stitch together the layers of felt with a straight stitch around each circle.

5. Referring to the circle 2 diagram, draw the smaller circle shapes onto the printed felt (CP). Repeat Step 2.

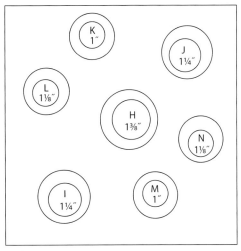

Circle 2

6. With the wrong side of the printed felt facing up, spray with Sulky KK 2000.

7. Place each cut square on the wrong side of the printed felt in this order:

  2¼" square cut from C2 behind H

  1¾" squares cut from C2 behind L and N

  2" squares cut from C3 behind I and J

  1¾" squares cut from C3 behind K and M

8. Repeat Step 4.

9. Fuse the 8⅞" × 8⅞" piece of interfacing to the wrong side of the front base.

EMBROIDERY AND EMBELLISHMENT

See Let's Get Started! (page 36) as needed, Index of Stitches (page 157) for page numbers, and Bead Embroidery and Bead Woven Stitches (page 45) for stitch directions.

See the placement and stitch diagrams (page 125) to complete the embroidery and embellishment.

ASSEMBLY

1. After you have added the embroidery and embellishment, place the back C1 piece of felt to the wrong side of the embroidered front. Pin together the 2 layers. Leave a 3″ opening along one side.

2. Stitch together the 2 layers with a whipstitch or straight stitch, using perle cotton. Stop at the opening.

3. Stuff the pillow, using a stuffing tool if needed.

4. Pin the opening closed. Repeat Step 2 to stitch the remaining section.

5. Stitch the looped edge stitch (page 72) around the outer edge of the pillow, using size 11° seed beads.

Felt circles: A & H, B & I, C & J, D & K, E & L, F & N, G & M
Button groups: 1–11
Use the photograph as a reference to work the stitches in the order they are listed.

BUTTON PLACEMENT

Button groups: 1, 2, 3, 4, 6 & 8	Button groups: 5, 7 & 9	Single buttons: 10 & 11
Large button Medium button Medium button	Large button Medium button Small button	Small button

Note: *Use the numbered sections on the photograph (previous page) for button placement. Stitch the buttons in place with perle cotton.*

EMBROIDERY STITCH DIAGRAM   *SB = seed bead*

Felt circles: A & H, Button group 1

Outer circle	Inner circle		Center: 11
Lazy daisy stitch fancy: 8° & 11° SBs	Bead combination stitch: Sequin and 8° & 11° SBs	Stacked bead stitch: 6° & 11° SBs	Button bezel stitch: 11° SBs

Large button	Medium button	Medium button
Stacked bead stitch: 8° & 11° SBs	Continuous bead stitch curved: 11° SBs	Stacked bead stitch: 8° & 11° SBs

Felt circles B & I, Button group 2; felt circles C & J, Button group 6

Outer circle	Inner circle			Center: 11
Double bubble stitch: 8° & 11° SBs	Bead cascade stitch: Sequin & 11° SBs	Bead cascade stitch: Sequin & 11° SBs	Bead combination stitch: 11° & 8° SBs	Button bezel stitch: 11° SBs

Large button	Medium button		Medium button
Stacked bead stitch: 8° & 11° SBs	Detail, stacked bead stitch: 6° & 11° SBs	Stacked bead stitch: 8° & 11° SBs	Continuous bead stitch curved: 11° SBs

Felt circles D & K, Button group 7; felt circles G & M, Button group 4

Outer circle	Inner circle			Center: 11
Stacked bead stitch: Sequin & 11° SB	Fly stitch: 11° SBs	Bead combination stitch: 11° & 8° SBs	Stacked bead stitch: 6° & 11° SBs	Button bezel stitch: 11° SBs

Large button	Medium button	Small or medium button
Stacked bead stitch: 6° & 11° SBs	Stacked bead stitch: 6° & 11° SBs	Continuous bead stitch curved: 11° SBs

Felt circles E & L, Button group 9; felt circles F & N, Button group 5

Outer circle		Inner circle			Center: 11
Continuous bead stitch fancy: 11° SBs	Stacked bead stitch: Sequin and 8° & 11° SBs	Picot tip stitch: Sequin & 11° SBs	Grouped bead stitch: 11° SBs	Single bead stitch: 8° SBs	Button bezel stitch: 11° SBs

Large button	Medium button	Small button
Stacked bead stitch: 8° & 11° SBs	Stacked bead stitch: 8° & 11° SBs	Continuous bead stitch curved: 11° SBs

Button group 3; Button group 8

Continuous bead stitch curved: 11° SBs	Stacked bead stitch: 6° & 11° SBs	Stacked bead stitch: 8° & 11° SBs

BEADED TANDLETONS

SKILL LEVEL: BEGINNER TO INTERMEDIATE

Project A: Miss Muffet, silk satin ribbon, finished size: 1¾" × 2½"

Miss Muffet with her Pretty Maids and Fair Misses

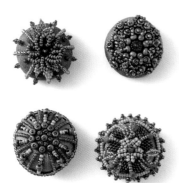

Project B: Pretty Maids, silk habotai bias ribbons, finished size: ¾" × 1½"

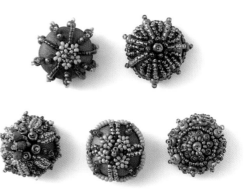

Project C: Fair Misses, silk habotai bias ribbons, finished size: ¾" × 1"

Tandletons: TAtted / NeeDLE lace / butTONS

"Tandletons" is the name I gave to a project that I created with a base made from a stuffed silk ribbon shape. Originally, my Tandletons were embroidered with threads, but for this book, I included examples stitched with bead embroidery and bead woven stitches. These little beaded treasures are truly a delight to make and can be used as baubles, brooches, or buttons.

Materials

The following materials will vary depending upon the size of the ribbon you have chosen for the base, design, and finishing.

Note: This project uses a silk bias ribbon that is made from silk habotai or silk satin fabric. The ribbon has a raw bias edge and a stitched seam about every 2 yards. Try to avoid using the seam in your base, as it can distort the form when you are stuffing it.

- 1 yard of silk satin or silk habotai bias ribbon in 2½", 1½", or 1" widths
- 1 spool of sewing thread
- 1 bobbin or card of beading thread
- Needles: Small sharps and beading
- Small amount of stuffing
- 1 package *each* of size 6° seed beads: 4 colors
- 1 package *each* of size 8° seed beads: 4 colors
- 1 package *each* of size 11° seed beads: 6 colors
- 1 package *each* of size 15° seed beads: 3 colors
- 1 package *each* of size 11° delica beads: 4 colors
- 1 strand beads, size 8 mm
- 1 strand beads, size 4 mm

Additional Items

- 1 button, size ½"
- Small scrap of felt
- 1" pin back
- Dome snap, size 2

Seed beads

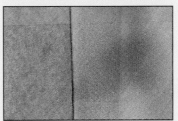

Ribbon

Other components

Embroidery Progression

The embroidery stitches are worked through the ribbon of the base. To begin a thread, come up through the bottom of the base to the point where the stitching will start.

The stitches are worked in sections, starting at the top of the base. A design can be worked in concentric horizontal circles or in vertical rows radiating from the center. After each row, the needle is threaded to the underside and then back to the beginning of the next row or ring.

To end a stitch or thread, go down through to the bottom of the base, knot, and cut the thread.

EMBROIDERY AND EMBELLISHMENT

See Let's Get Started! (page 36) as needed, Index of Stitches (page 157) for page numbers, and Bead Embroidery and Bead Woven Stitches (page 45) for stitch directions.

See Project A: Miss Muffet (page 129), Project B: Pretty Maids (page 130), or Project C: Fair Misses (page 131) for embroidery and embellishment for each project.

CREATING THE TANDLETON BASE

Examples of 1" and 1½" ribbon base

Measure and Cut

Ribbon width	Cut 1 length per base.
2½"	8¾"
1½"	5¼"
1"	3½"
⅝"	2³⁄₁₆"

1. Fold the ribbon length in half, right side in, matching the raw edges.

2. Anchor knot the sewing thread ⅛" from the raw edges. Stitch together the raw edges with an ⅛" seam allowance. Anchor knot the thread.

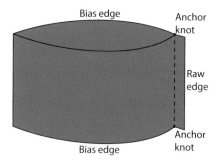

Bias edge

Anchor knot

Raw edge

Anchor knot

Bias edge

3. Starting at the seam, gather stitch through 1 layer of ribbon along the continuous edge back to the seam.

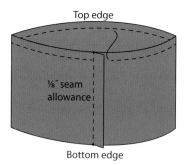

Top edge

⅛" seam allowance

Bottom edge

4. Gently pull the thread to close the top. Anchor knot the thread into the raw edges of the seam and cut the thread.

5. Turn the piece and repeat Step 3 on the other edge.

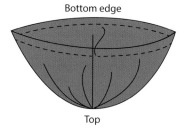

Bottom edge

Top

6. Gather the thread slightly. Roll some stuffing into a ball and insert it into the opening. The form should be fairly firm.

7. Pull in the gathers firmly. Anchor knot and cut the thread.

✿ Tip: Consistent-Sized Bases

If you are creating a group of buttons, I suggest that you section off equal amounts of stuffing for each base. This way, you ensure that the bases will all be of similar size and shape. Also note that the shape of the stuffed base may flatten and change once the stitching begins.

PROJECT A: MISS MUFFET

1. Follow the directions for Creating the Tandleton Base (previous page), using 2½"-wide ribbon.

2. Refer to Embroidery Progression (page 127).

3. Follow the directions for Finishing the Base, Bauble (below).

Use the photograph as a reference to work the stitches in the order they are listed.

| **EMBROIDERY STITCH DIAGRAM** | *SB = seed bead* |

First section: Circular	
1. Button: Stitch with beading thread.	2. Button sunflower stitch: 8° SB, 11° delica bead, 4 mm round bead & 15° SBs

Second section: Circular, horizontal
3. Lazy daisy stitch fancy: 8° & 11° SBs

Third section: Vertical			
Row 1		Row 2	
4. Stacked bead stitch: 6° & 11° SBs	5. Continuous bead stitch straight: 11° SBs	6. Stacked bead stitch: 8° & 15° SBs	7. Simple leaf stitch—medium: 11° delica beads

FINISHING THE BASE

Bauble

1. Cut a piece of felt slightly smaller than the bottom of the finished base.

2. Glue the felt to the wrong side of the bottom edge of the base with tacky glue.

Put the baubles in a bowl and admire your creative work!

Brooch

1. Follow Finishing the Base, Bauble, Step 1 (at left).

2. Hand stitch a 1" pin back to the felt with sewing thread.

Button with Snap

1. Follow Finishing the Base, Bauble, Step 1 (at left).

2. Hand stitch one part of a dome snap to the felt and the corresponding part to a blouse or jacket.

PROJECT B: PRETTY MAIDS

1. Follow the directions for Creating the Tandleton Base (page 128), using 1½″-wide ribbon.

2. Refer to Embroidery Progression (page 127).

3. Follow the directions for Finishing the Base, Brooch (page 129).

Variation 1: Use the photograph as a reference to work the stitches in the order they are listed.

EMBROIDERY STITCH DIAGRAM	SB = seed bead
First and second sections: Circular, horizontal	
1. Single bead stitch: 8 mm bead	2. Bead cascade stitch: 6° & 11° SBs
Third and fourth sections: Circular, horizontal	
3. Stacked bead stitch: 6° & 11° SBs	4. Continuous bead stitch curved: 11° SBs
Fifth and sixth sections: Circular, horizontal	
5. Stacked bead stitch: 6° & 11° SBs	6. Continuous bead stitch curved: 11° SBs
Seventh and eighth sections: Circular, horizontal	
7. Stacked bead stitch: 6° & 11° SBs	8. Continuous bead stitch curved: 11° SBs

Variation 2: Use the photograph as a reference to work the stitches in the order they are listed.

EMBROIDERY STITCH DIAGRAM	SB = seed bead
First section: Center	
1. Stacked bead stitch: 8° & 11° SBs	
Second section: Circular, horizontal	
2. Lazy daisy stitch fancy (loose): 8° & 11° SBs	3. Simple leaf stitch—medium: 11° delica beads
Third section: Vertical	
4. Continuous bead stitch straight: 11° SBs	5. Stacked bead stitch: 8° & 15° SBs

PROJECT C: FAIR MISSES

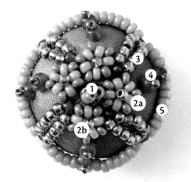

Variation 1: Use the photograph as a reference to work the stitches in the order they are listed.

1. Follow the directions for Creating the Tandleton Base (page 128), using 1"-wide ribbon

2. Refer to Embroidery Progression (page 127).

3. Follow the directions for Finishing the Base, Button with Snap (page 129).

EMBROIDERY STITCH DIAGRAM	*SB = seed bead*	
First and second sections: Circular, horizontal		
1. Picot tip stitch: 6° & 11° SBs	2a. Simple flower stitch: 2 colors of 11° SBs	2b. Center, single bead stitch: 11° SBs
Third section: Vertical		
3. Lazy daisy stitch fancy: 2 colors of 11° SBs		4. Stacked bead stitch: 8° & 15° SBs
Fourth section: Circular, horizontal		
5. Continuous bead stitch curved: 11° SBs		

Variation 2: Use the photograph as a reference to work the stitches in the order they are listed.

EMBROIDERY STITCH DIAGRAM	*SB = seed bead*	
First and second sections: Circular, horizontal		
1. Group of 5 beaded pistil stitches: 11° SBs, 4mm round bead & 15° SBs		2. Stacked bead stitch: 6° & 11° SBs
Third section: Vertical		
Row 1		Row 2
3. Stacked bead stitch: 8° & 15° SBs	4. Stacked bead stitch: 6° & 11° SBs	5. Lazy daisy stitch fancy: 2 colors of 11° SBs
Fourth section: Circular, horizontal		
6. Continuous bead stitch curved: 11° SBs		

CQ SEWING CADDY

SKILL LEVEL: INTERMEDIATE TO ADVANCED

Ivory and Pastel, finished size: 6″ × 7¾″

This handy little sewing caddy is the perfect size to store all your essential tools. The base is first crazy pieced with several different fabrics, with the bead embroidery and other embellishments following the pieced lines and open areas of fabric.

Pincushion and needle keep

The pincushion is a version of the Tandletons (page 126) using a 2½″-wide silk satin ribbon. Use perle cotton to create the sections and sew the button in the center. The needle keep is made from a 5″ × 4½″ piece of felt that is folded in half and machine stitched around the edges.

Additional Inspiration

In this version of the project, I used a larger piece of muslin for the foundation and made it into a wallhanging.

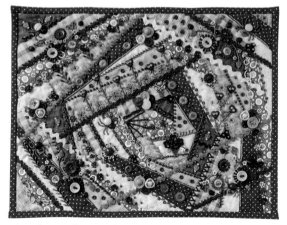

Primarily Crazy for Kevin, finished size: 15½″ × 20″

Materials

Note: All fabric measurements are based on 40"-wide fabric.

- 6 fat quarters (18" × 22") of fabric in monochromatic prints (A, B, C, D, E, F)
- ½ yard of coordinating fabric for lining, pockets, and binding (G)
- ¼ yard of muslin for foundation
- ¼ yard of midweight interfacing (such as Pellon 931TD Fusible Midweight)
- 1 yard of ½" flat lace trim
- 1 yard of ⅜" flat lace trim
- 1 spool of decorative sewing machine thread
- 1 spool of sewing thread
- 1 bobbin or card of beading thread
- Needles: Topstitching for machine, small sharps, and beading
- 1 package *each* of size 6° seed beads: 6 colors
- 1 package *each* of size 8° seed beads: 4 colors
- 1 package *each* of size 11° seed beads: 7 colors
- 1 package *each* of size 15° seed beads: 3 colors
- 1 package *each* of bugle beads: 3 colors
- 1 button for front decoration
- 2 dome snaps, size 2
- 34 mother-of-pearl buttons in a variety of sizes
- 2 shank buttons, size ⅜", for spiders
- 2 sew-through buttons, size ¼", for spiders
- 5 charms, size 10 mm
- 3 glass flower rondelles, size 10 mm
- 9 glass beads, size 8 mm
- 3 tulip beads, size 8 mm
- 6 tulip beads, size 6 mm
- 12 flower buttons, size 6 mm
- 3 flower rondelles, size 5 mm
- 11 flower rondelles, size 4 mm

Other components

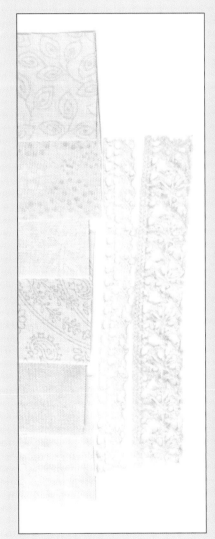

Fabric and lace trim

Seed and bugle beads

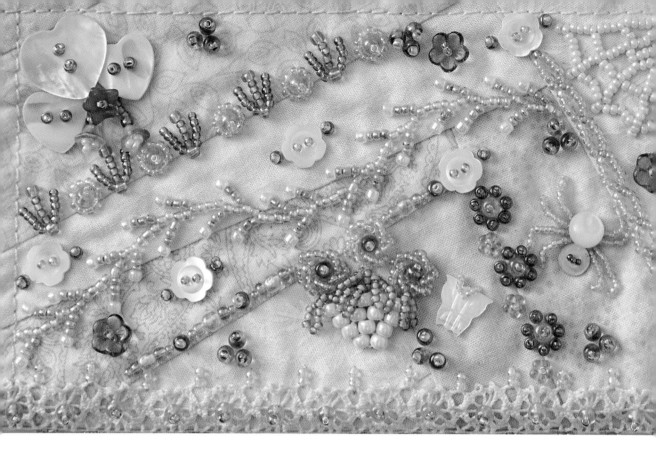

Cutting

From fabric color G:

- 1 piece 7½″ × 16½″
- 1 piece 7½″ × 10″
- 1 piece 7½″ × 9″
- 1 piece 1″ × 7½″
- 2 pieces 3″ × 16½″
- 2 pieces 3″ × 9½″

From ⅜″ flat lace trim:

- 1 piece 7″ (AL)
- 1 piece 5½″ (BL)
- 2 pieces 7½″ (CL)

From the fat quarters:

Note: First cut the fat quarter pieces of fabric in half to measure 9″ × 22″.

- From color A: 4 wedges ½″ × 1½″ × 9″
- From color B: 4 strips 1½″ × 9″
- From color C: 4 wedges ¾″ × 2″ × 9″
- From color D: 4 strips 1¾″ × 9″
- From color E: 4 wedges 1″ × 2½″ × 9″
- From color F: 4 strips 2″ × 9″

From the other materials:

- 1 piece of muslin 8″ × 17″
- 2 pieces of midweight interfacing 7½″ × 16½″
- 2 pieces of ½″ flat lace trim, 7½″ each (DL)

SEWING

1. Fold the muslin in half to find the center.

2. Cut a 2″ × 2½″ piece from a strip F; pin this in the center of the muslin. Place the next piece with right sides together and raw edges matching. Machine stitch with a ¼″ seam allowance.

3. Fold the fabric open and press the seam flat. Trim any excess fabric even with the previous fabric.

4. Follow the piecing diagram for the piecing order.

5. Trim the base to 16½″ long × 7½″ wide.

6. Fuse the 16½″ × 7½″ piece of interfacing to the wrong side of the muslin base.

7. Use a chalk pencil to measure and draw a line 5½″ from the right end and 4½″ from the left end. Measure and draw a ¾″ line from each raw edge.

8. Machine stitch along the drawn lines with a decorative thread.

9. Place the 7″ (AL) and 5½″ (BL) pieces of lace according to the diagram. Hand stitch in place with sewing thread. Trim off any excess lace.

10. Place the straight edges of the remaining pieces of lace (DL and CL) along the machine-stitched vertical lines. Hand stitch in place with sewing thread.

11. Machine stitch a basting stitch ¼″ from the raw edges.

Optional: Place a line of Fray Check on all the raw edges.

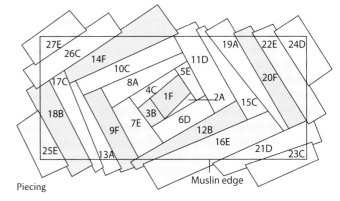

Piecing

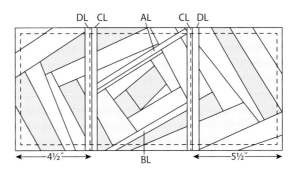

EMBROIDERY AND EMBELLISHMENT

See Let's Get Started! (page 36) as needed, Index of Stitches (page 157) for page numbers, and Bead Embroidery and Bead Woven Stitches (page 45) for stitch directions.

Front Flap

Use the photograph as a reference to work the stitches in the order they are listed.

EMBROIDERY STITCH DIAGRAM   *SB = seed bead*

Button group A		
Button hole decoration stitches: 11° & 15° SBs	Single bead stitch: Flower button	Bead combination stitch: 8° & 11° SBs

Button group B	
Button hole decoration stitches: 11° & 15° SBs	Single bead stitch: Flower button

Button group C	
Button hole decoration stitches: 11° & 15° SBs	Front-to-back hole charm stitch: Butterfly charm & 15° SBs

Button D			
Button hole decoration stitches: 15° SBs	Stem, continuous bead stitch: 11° SBs	Lazy daisy stitch: 11° SBs	Stacked bead stitch: 8° & 15° SBs
1. French rose stitch: 8°, 11° & 15° SBs	2. Lazy daisy stitch with loop: 11° SBs		3. Stacked bead stitch: Tulip bead & 11° SB
4. Top-to-bottom hole charm dangle stitch: Tulip bead and 8° & 11° SBs	5. Row, stacked bead stitch: 6° & 11° SBs		6. Feather stitch: 11° SBs
7. Single bead stitch: 11° SBs	8. Flower with petite petals, stacked bead stitch: 8° & 15° SBs		9. Bead combination stitch: 8° & 11° SBs
10. Jacks stitch: 8° & 11° SBs	11. Stacked bead stitch: 6° & 11° SBs		12. Continuous bead stitch curved: 11° SBs
13. Stacked bead stitch: 8° & 15° SBs	14. Lazy daisy stitch fancy, border row/ split spaced: 8° & 11° SBs		15. Single bead stitch: 8° SBs
16. Stacked bead stitch: 6° & 11° SBs	17. Blanket stitch angled & frilled: Bugle beads and 11° & 8° SBs		18. Stacked bead stitches: 6° & 11° SBs
19a. Floret star stitch: 2 colors of 11° SBs	19b. Center, stacked bead stitch: 6° & 11° SBs		20. Button flower with petals stitch, stacked bead stitch: 8° & 11° SBs
21. Single bead stitch: Flower button	22. Lazy daisy stitch: 11° SBs		23a. Simple flower stitch: 11° SBs
23b. Center, single bead stitch: 11° SBs	24. Stacked bead stitch: Flower rondelle & 11° SBs		25. Stacked bead stitch: 6° & 11° SBs
26. Stacked bead stitch: 6° & 11° SBs	27. Grouped bead stitch: 11° SBs		28. Grouped bead stitch: 11° SBs

Back Section

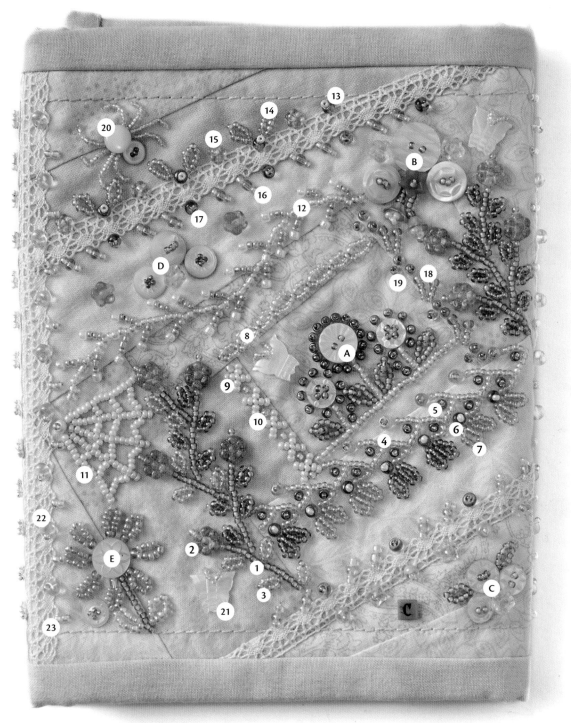

Use the photograph as a reference to work the stitches in the order they are listed.

EMBROIDERY STITCH DIAGRAM   *SB = seed bead*

Button group A

Row and flower stem, continuous bead stitch: 11° SBs	Button hole decoration stitches: 11° SBs	Button flower with petals stitch, stacked bead stitch: 8° & 15° SBs	Lazy daisy stitch with loop: 11° SBs

Button group B

Button hole decoration stitches: 11° SBs	Stacked bead stitch: Tulip bead & 11° SB	Top-to-bottom hole charm dangle stitch: Tulip bead and 8° & 11° SBs	Single bead stitch: Flower button

Button group C

Button hole decoration stitches: 11° SBs	Lazy daisy stitch: 11° SBs	Single bead stitch: Flower button

Button group D

Button hole decoration stitches: 11° & 15° SBs	Single bead stitch: Flower button

Button group E

Button hole decoration stitches: 11° & 15° SBs	Stem, continuous bead stitch: 11° SBs	Button flower with petals stitch, lazy daisy stitch fancy: 8° & 11° SBs	Lazy daisy stitch: 11° SBs

1. Continuous bead stitch curved: 11° SBs	2. Side-to-side hole charm stitch: Flower bead & 11° SBs	3. Lazy daisy stitch: 2 colors of 11° SBs
4. Feather stitch: 11° SBs	5. Stacked bead stitch: 8° & 15° SBs	6. Stacked bead stitch: 2 colors each of 6° & 11° SBs
7. Lazy daisy stitch: 2 colors of 11° SBs	8. Chain stitch long-short: 11° SBs	9. Cross stitch row: 11° SBs
10. Single bead stitch: 11° SBs	11. Spider web stitch: 6° & 11° SBs	12. Blanket stitch angled & fancy: 11° & 8° SBs
13. Stacked bead stitch: 6° & 11° SBs	14. Lazy daisy stitch border rows / split spaced: 11° SBs	15. Stacked bead stitch: Flower rondelle & 11° SB
16. Bead combination stitch: 8° & 11° SBs	17. Stacked bead stitch: 6° & 11° SBs	18. Bead combination stitch: 11° & 8° SBs
19. Stacked bead stitch: 8° & 15° SBs	20. Spider stitch: Buttons & 15° SBs	21. Front-to-back hole charm stitch: Butterfly charm & 15° SBs
22. Stacked bead stitch: 6° & 11° SBs	23. Grouped bead stitch: 11° SBs	

Pocket

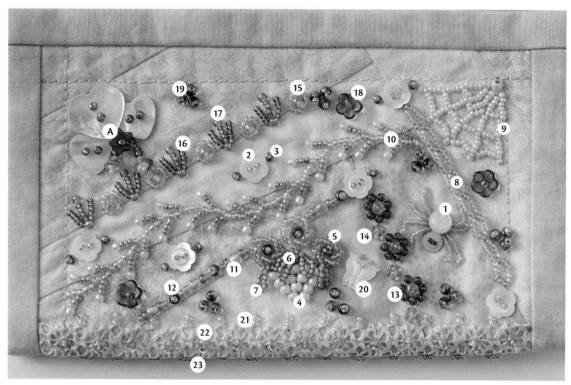

Use the photograph as a reference to work the stitches in the order they are listed.

EMBROIDERY STITCH DIAGRAM   *SB = seed bead*

Button group A		
Button hole decoration stitches: 8° & 15° SBs	Stacked bead stitch: Tulip bead & 11° SB	Top-to-bottom hole charm dangle stitch: Tulip bead and 8° & 11° SBs
1. Spider stitch: Buttons & 15° SBs	2. Button hole decoration stitches: 11° SBs	3. Stacked bead stitch: 8° & 11° SBs
4. Basket stitch: 6° SBs	5. Small French rose stitch: 6° & 11° SBs	6. Stem, continuous bead stitch: 11° SBs
7. Lazy daisy stitch: 11° SBs	8. Chain stitch: 11° SBs	9. Spider web stitch: 6° & 11° SBs
10. Blanket stitch angled & fancy: 11° & 8° SBs	11. Bead combination stitch: 11°, 8° & 6° SBs	12. Stacked bead stitch: 6° & 11° SBs
13. Flower with petite petals, stacked bead stitch: 6°, 8°, 11° & 15° SBs	14. Stacked bead stitch: Flower rondelle & 11° SBs	15. Floret stitch: 6° & 11° SBs
16. Fly stitch: 11° & 8° SBs	17. Bead combination stitch: 11° & 8° SBs	18. Picot tip stitch: Flower bead & 15° SBs
19. Stacked bead stitch: 6° & 11° SBs	20. Front-to-back hole charm stitch: Butterfly charm & 15° SBs	21. Grouped bead stitch: 11° SBs
22. Stacked bead stitch: 6° & 11° SBs		23. Grouped bead stitch: 11° SBs

ASSEMBLY

1. If needed, press the embroidered front from the wrong side to remove any wrinkles in the fabrics.

2. Fuse the remaining 7½″ × 16½″ piece of interfacing to the wrong side of the 7½″ × 16½″ piece of fabric G for the lining.

3. Place the lining right side up.

4. Fold and press the 7½″ × 9″ piece of fabric to make a piece 7½″ × 4½″. Fold and press the 7½″ × 10″ piece of fabric to make a piece 7½″ × 5″.

5. Pin the raw edges of the 7½″ × 4½″ folded piece of fabric to the raw edges of the right edge of the lining.

6. Machine baste the raw edge in place. Machine stitch down the center with decorative thread.

7. Mark a line 4½″ in from the raw edges of the left edge of the lining. Pin the raw edges of the 7½″ × 5″ folded piece of fabric on this line. Repeat Step 6.

8. Fold and press the long edges of the 1″ × 7½″ piece of fabric to the center to make a piece ½″ × 7½″. Pin over the raw edges of the 7½″ × 5″ folded piece of fabric. Machine stitch in place with decorative thread.

9. Place the lining right side down. Place the embroidered base right side up on top of the lining. Pin together the layers.

10. Machine baste around the raw edges with a ¼″ seam allowance.

11. Fold the width of the 2 pieces of fabric 3″ × 16½″ in half. Press the fold.

12. Pin the raw edges of the folded 16½″ strips even with the long edges of the embroidered base.

13. Follow Bouquet of Flowers, Assembly, Steps 6–8 (page 90).

14. Fold the width of the 2 pieces of fabric 3″ × 9½″ in half. Press the fold.

15. Pin the raw edges of the folded 9½″ strips even with the short edges of the embroidered base.

16. Repeat Step 13, tucking in and hand stitching the ends and the fold.

17. On the left end, sew dome snaps in the corners and 8¼″ from the corners to create an open pocket.

4½″   5″   4½″   Fold   Fold

GALLERY

BODY ADORNMENTS

Grapevine Bracelet, 7½" × 1¼"

The base of the bracelet is made from seed beads and square beads, with bead woven grapes and leaves made from seed and delica beads.

Flowers and Peas Bracelet, 8¾" × 1"

The base of the bracelet is made from seed beads, with bead woven pea pods, flowers, and leaves made from seed and delica beads.

Pea Pod Bracelet, 8" × 1"

This bracelet is made from bead woven pea pods that are linked together with glass buttons and larger beads.

Spiral Vine Bracelet, 9" × 1¼"

The base of the bracelet is made from seed beads and larger glass beads, with bead woven leaves made from seed beads.

 Tip: Beaded Charms

If you want to make a peyote- or brick-stitched form into a charm like the leaves in this bracelet, bury the tails back through the outer edges and body of the stitch. Then attach using any of the charm techniques in Bead Embroidery and Bead Woven Stitches (page 45).

The base of the bracelet is made from grosgrain ribbon, and the pansies are made from French wire ribbon. Both the bracelet and the pansies are embellished with the looped edge stitch.

Pansy Bracelet, 7½″ × 2¾″

The base of the bracelet is made from velvet ribbon, embellished with bead woven flowers and leaves, glass flowers, leaves, and larger beads.

Rose Garden Bracelet, 7¾″ × 1½″

This is a version of the Beaded Bracelets project (page 108), with the buttons stitched with flower petals, smaller glass buttons, large glass beads, and flower rondelles.

Gray Roses Bracelet, 7½″ × 1⅞″

This is a version of the Beaded Bracelets project (page 108), with the buttons in two sizes, as well as large glass beads, small flower buttons, and glass leaves.

Victorian Garden Bracelet, 7½″ × 1⅞″

FADED MEMORIES

8⅝" × 10¼"

The base of this wallhanging started with a vintage embroidered purse. The ruffled silk edges are adorned with vintage shell, metal, and celluloid buttons; metal charms; and ribbonwork posies, leaves, and butterflies. Bead woven leaves and dragonflies adorn the center section.

FRIPPERY

Cotillion Tassel 1, 11¼″ × 2″   Cotillion Tassel 2, 13″ × 2″

Jellyfish Tassel 1, 7″ × 2″   Jellyfish Tassel 2, 7″ × 2″

The base of the Cotillion Tassel is a cork covered with tapestry fabric and adorned with velvet leaves, glass flowers, and shell charms. The three outer tassel legs are made from a jacquard ribbon; the six inner legs are made from a silk rouleau cord wound with a rococo trim. The legs are embroidered with seed beads, larger glass beads, and metal and shell charms.

The base of the Jellyfish Tassel is velvet ribbon that is stitched with the same technique as the Beaded Tandletons (page 126). A cord is inserted into the top before closing the stitches. The embroidered base is worked with seed beads and larger glass beads. The dangles are worked with seed beads, larger beads, and charms.

PANSIES AND SUNFLOWERS SCRAP ROLL

3½″ × 3″ (closed) or 3½″ × 34″ (opened)

This is a slightly simpler version of the Scrap Roll (page 114). I used larger buttons, appliqués, and rosettes, as well as wider trims for the base. These sections are embellished with bead embroidery. The button flowers have a floral wire stem and are clustered together with more wire. I used this group for the center of the roll instead of a wooden spool.

SPIDERS AND WEBS

Pearly Spider Brooch, 2⅝″ round

Spooky Spider Brooch, 2⅝″ round

These are examples of the Beaded Brooches project (page 94). I embroidered the stylized web using a smaller version of the pattern included in the Spider's Webs project (page 102).

This is a version of the Spider's Webs project (page 102). The web covers the entire square, and the spokes are worked in the free-form peyote stitch fuller row using beads including hex, triangular, delica, and seed. Bead woven leaves and flowers are worked throughout the web.

Along Came a Spider, 9″ × 9″

BEADED TREASURES

Flower Pot Brooches,
1½" × 1"

Bitty Beaded
Bag, 8⅛" × 4"

This little treasure is made from cotton batik fabric, satin ribbon, and silk rouleau cord. The bead embroidery follows the pattern of the satin ribbons.

These dainty little brooches begin with the brick stitch basket stitch (page 83). Beads and charms were added to create the flowers.

Sweet Caroline, 5" × 5½"

Midnight Serenade Brooch, 2⅛" × 3"

This little pouch has a base made from silk and lace scraps, plus a shibori dyed silk habotai fabric. The beads are worked in vignettes, vines, and border row sections.

This is an example of the Beaded Brooches project (page 94). Small bits of lace and buttons adorn the fabric and are embroidered with a variety of beads.

BEAUTIFUL BEADED BLOOMS

13″ × 13″

The base of this wallhanging started with two colors of moiré fabric. The opulent beading follows the seams of the fabric and the embroidered bead frames. Glass buttons were used as the center of many of the flowers.

MOTHER NATURE'S GIFTS

Bird Song
Necklace,
14″ × 4″

Dragonfly Tropics, 4″ × 2¾″

The base of this brooch begins with a wire-and-batting form that is covered in silk bias ribbon. The large embellishments include silk ribbonwork flowers, a bead woven dragonfly and leaves, glass flowers, and abalone buttons.

The center piece of the necklace is made from collage silk and cotton fabrics. It is embroidered with a shisha mirror, buttons, charms, and beads. The necklace is made from cord, covered in the circular peyote stitch.

Dragonfly Moon,
4″ × 3¼″

The base of this brooch is a carved mother-of-pearl shell. The dragonfly is made from a dentalium shell, with a bead woven body and wings. Bead woven leaves, shell charms, and glass beads dangle below.

TIDAL POOLS

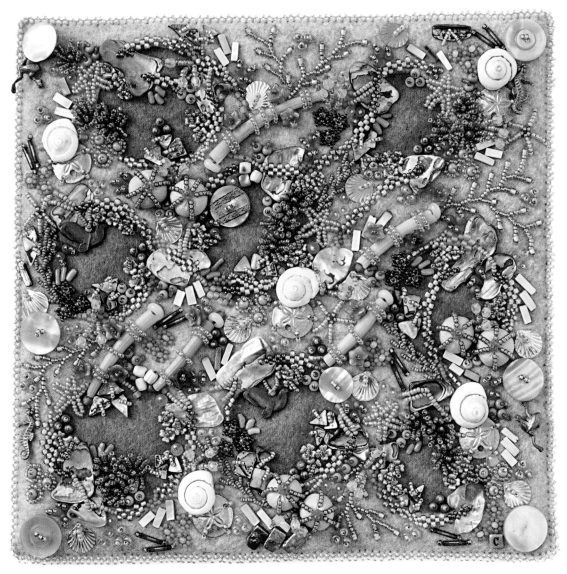

9″ × 9″

This is a variation of the Blowing Bubbles project (page 121), with only two colors of felt. The "pools" are filled with starfish and anemone and are encrusted in the free-form peyote stitch. Small Tandletons (⅝″ ribbon), as in the Beaded Tandletons (page 126), were stitched to resemble sea urchins.

BEADS AND MORE BEADS

This is another example of the Beadazzled Stitches class (page 15) that I taught online. This base was strip pieced and backed with Décor-Bond interfacing for stability. The lines of the seams and open spaces are embroidered with the majority of the stitches included in this book.

Sizzle and Pop, 15¾″ × 15⅞″

In this variation of the Blowing Bubbles project (page 121), a printed felt is used for the base, with the embroidery following the print's design. Vintage and new buttons were used to add color and focal points.

Cogs and Gears, 9¼″ × 9¼″

BEADAZZLED SOMEMORE PURSE

This purse begins with a machine-quilted batik fabric. The embroidery is worked in the free-form peyote stitch, with large beads and charms added in here and there.

7½" × 7"

Back

VARIATION ON A THEME

These two wallhangings are versions of the Bouquet of Flowers project A from Feminine Fancies (page 86). Buttons were used for the focal flowers and frame.

Champagne and Pearls, 10⅜″ × 10⅜″

Welcome Home, 10½″ × 10½″

EASTERN INFLUENCES

17½″ × 16¾″

This piece started with the small scrap of fabric that I used for the center. Solid and printed cotton fabrics were used for the strip-pieced frame and border. Glass seed and bugle beads were used in the embroidery; additional embellishments are vintage buttons, sequins, and large glass charms and beads.

WILD PERSIMMONS

13½" × 13½"

This piece started with a crazy-pieced base of silk and cotton fabrics, which was machine quilted in a random spiral pattern. Vintage plastic and glass buttons, sequins, glass seed beads, and larger glass beads were used for the embroidery and embellishments.

INDEX OF STITCHES

Sizzle and Pop (page 152)

ABOUT THE AUTHOR

CHRISTEN BROWN was born in Manhattan Beach, California, and spent her formative years in Torrance, California. She first became interested in fiber arts via making clothing for her dolls as a child. After graduating from high school, she continued her education at the Fashion Institute of Design & Merchandising in Los Angeles, California, where she graduated with an associate of arts in fashion design.

Christen began her career in the wearable art field in 1986. Her work has been shown in galleries and fashion shows all over the world. She has been invited to participate in both the Fairfield and BERNINA Fashion Shows. She has had her work included in *The Costume Maker's Art*, *The Button Craft Book*, *Michael's Arts & Crafts* magazine, *Martha Stewart Weddings* magazine, and *Visions: Quilts of a New Decade* (by C&T Publishing). She has written a human-interest article for *Threads* magazine and has had several historical articles published by *Piecework* magazine.

Christen began teaching and presenting her work in 1991, starting with one local store. She quickly became a permanent addition to the teaching staff of several stores in Southern California. She has also taught for quilt and fiber art guilds on the West Coast, and she has been invited to teach nationally for Road to California, American Quilter's Society, and Quilt Festival Houston.

Christen's published titles for C&T Publishing include *Ribbonwork Gardens*, *Embroidered & Embellished*, *Ribbonwork Flowers*, *The Embroidery Book*, and *Embroidery Stitching Handy Pocket Guide*. She also has a line of templates: fast2mark Embroidery Stencils, Essential Collection.

Christen continues to be interested in craft and fine art. She experiments and learns all that she can, specifically concentrating on design and the techniques of embroidery, quilting, ribbonwork, mixed media, and beadwork. Her goal and wish through this journey is to continually be surprised, inspired, creative, and necessary. You can contact her through her website.

Visit Christen online and follow on social media!

Website
christenbrown.com

Blog
1creativeone.wordpress.com

Facebook
/christenjbrown

Pinterest
/christenjbrown

Also by Christen Brown:

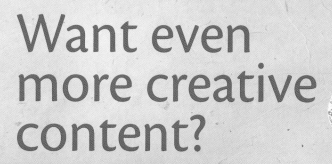

Want even more creative content?

Go to ctpub.com/offer

& sign up to receive our gift to you!

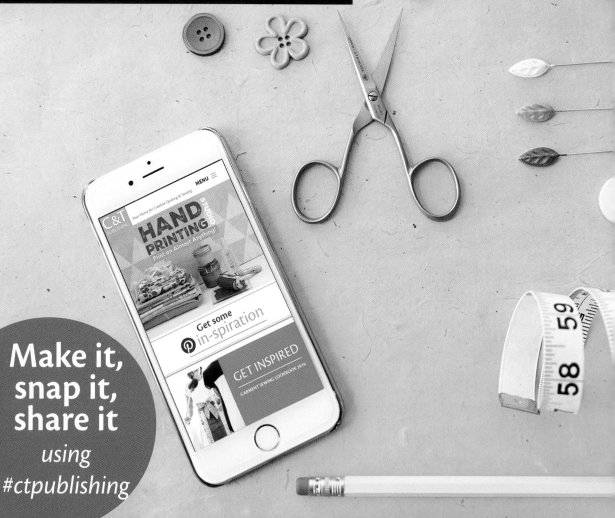

Make it, snap it, share it *using #ctpublishing*